Dividend Investing During Inflation

How to Set-Up a World-Class Dividend Portfolio

Kendrick Fernandez

Table of Contents

Introduction

"Do you know the only thing that gives me pleasure? It's to see my dividends coming in."

This is amazing proverb, and guess who said this? Someone just as great... **John D. Rockefeller**.

Dividend investing has been an overlooked term in an age of booming tech startups, mega FAANG overreach and cryptos exploding to the moon.

Have you heard anyone say the following? **Dividends are booring man. I'm going to the moon. Have fun staying poor.**

Well, Dividend Investing is not for everyone. It's for those with patience. It's for those who love passive income. Dividend investing is one of the simplest investment strategies to understand and is a great way for beginners to start investing. It is a low-risk way of investing, ideal for risk-averse investors. This investment strategy focuses on maximizing the benefits of dividends, whether they are reinvested or used otherwise.

So why dividend stocks during inflation? Investing during inflation is a treacherous pursuit. People, families, small business, large business, everything and everyone is fighting against rising expenses. At the same time, everyone is reducing their spending. Businesses are losing revenue. People are getting unemployed. Margins getting crushed.

There's one thing that can help people stay above ground in such a situation. **Income!!!**

Income from your job, income from investments, royalty income, business income.

Income can be increased with increase in inflation.

Income that keeps pace with inflation is like oxygen on the moon. It needs to be treasured, studied and replicated.

Dividend income is one such income. It is one of the simplest forms of income that you control, and that can increase with inflation. If you follow the advice in this book, and buy the right stocks at the right time, it is one way to protect yourself.

The best protection is a job whose income increases with inflation. The second best is dividend income.

It's like the shield that will protect you and your family while the inflation dragon is breathing down on you.

Once the inflation dragon runs out of fire and collapses, you can resume your journey to stronger financial times.

Bitcoin, Google, Amazon..... There's a lot of hype there, but they pay no dividend. The bigger they are, the harder they can fall during an inflationary collapse.

The tortoise will beat the hair.

Get ready to jump on the dividend tortoise.

This book contains an introduction to inflation investing and then nine chapters after that. Each chapter is dedicated to a significant aspect of dividend investing, with detailed descriptions and examples. At the end of each chapter is a quiz that acts as a summary of the chapter. The questions are designed to check if you understood the concepts in the chapter. If you are able to answer all the questions in the chapter, then you have a strong understanding of the concept and are able to move ahead.

Investing During Inflation

Inflation Defined

So, what is inflation?

Inflation is when you paid $15 for a $10 haircut you used to get for $5 when you had hair. This hilarious quote, by former baseball star Sam Ewing, summarizes inflation better than the Harvard economists who always fail to predict inflation.

The inflation crisis of 2021-2022 is similar to a lot of previous inflation crises that have plagued the world. It starts with excessive government printing of money in response to an external crisis like a war, famine or pandemic. Or maybe sometimes just a lazy unproductive population.

Inflation is defined as the general rise in the prices of goods and services in an economy. The inflation rate is, therefore, the rate at which that change happens. When inflation goes up, it implies that whatever you are buying has become more expensive. This reduces the buyer's purchasing power, and they can buy less. This is a huge problem for many investors, and many are left wondering how to fight this. Here's how you can go about it.

You must fight inflation head-on if you intend to safeguard your long-term investments. Inflation is a long-term problem, and it will always be there.

On the other hand, inflation is an opportunity. There are ways to take advantage of inflation to benefit from inflation.

While detailed methods to fight inflation are beyond the scope of this book, we will mention some of these principles in this chapter.

There is nothing better than an investment strategy that helps make inflation work for you. The inflation mechanism that increases the prices of goods and services is the same mechanism through which company profits increase. There is a hidden advantage to inflation proofed investing. This is the advantage of pricing power. Most world-class companies have pricing power which allows them to sell more products to more people at high prices. If certain companies were to hike their prices the same way, they would witness a great decline in sales because they do not have the same pricing power.

The demand for the goods and services of companies with pricing power does not decline with increases in prices. People will not be prompted to let go of their favorite product because of a slight increase in price. Great businesses that have durable competitive advantages like intellectual property and brand recognition have pricing power. The durability of the advantages that these companies have make dividend investing a long-term solution for inflation. A rising tide lifts all boats. Inflation-proof investments are like a rising tide on which all lifeboats float, but for you to survive, you must be on a lifeboat.

The lifeboat in this book is dividend investing. Other strategies you can use involve investing in previous metals, commodities, currency diversification, real estate with fixed long-term debt, investing in high cash flow businesses, REITS etc.

If you're interested in a book focused on a broader approach to inflation investing, you can check out my book on Inflation Investing here.

https://www.amazon.com/gp/product/B08WJZCTPV/

But now, let's get back to Dividend Investing....

Pros/Cons of Dividend Stocks During Inflation

Dividend investing has its fair share of advantages and disadvantages. It's best to have a strong understanding of both, before you dive in.

Advantages

- Dividend investing makes it possible to invest passive income and to increase share ownership. The reinvestment of funds means that each time there is reinvestment, the number of shares held also increases. If paid out in cash, the dividends can also be collected as supplementary income.

- Dividend investing helps you gain capital without using your savings or getting into debt. You can grow your portfolio without having to worry about borrowing from brokers whose rates are very high. You also do not need to make any out-of-pocket expenses to buy shares to increase your holdings. The system is self-propagating.

- Your portfolio is less subject to volatility and is very stable. Most people invest in dividend-paying companies for the long term. So, they are unlikely to sell into volatility, like growth stocks. You will have less sleepless nights worrying about your portfolio. Low volatility also directly translates to lower risk.

- Stockowners are rewarded for their long-term holdings because dividend investing holds the prospect of rising dividends.

- Dividend investors pay fewer taxes in comparison to investors who engage in frequent trading. Dividend payments are taxed as regular income in most countries instead of capital gains. In certain countries, tax free dividends are common.

- Dividend investments are a good hedge against inflation because they are very stable.

- High-yield dividend investors have the advantage of profiting from their investments in bear markets. If the dividends payouts are not cut, they continue to receive income.

Disadvantages

- Dividend stocks have lower growth potential. Their level of appreciation is, therefore, lower than that of inflation. They then can get engulfed by the prices soaring higher at a faster rate.

- Dividend investing requires you to set aside some of the money you receive to pay taxes. These investments are taxed at the long capital gains rate. In the case that you hold your stocks in an account that is tax-deferred, you will not have to pay taxes in the year the dividends are received.

- A long-time horizon is required for a dividend investing strategy. It is not ideal for investors who start investing later in life. They may outlive their investments and will not be able to maximize their returns.

- When you sell a dividend investing stock, you cut off the income that you were receiving from that stock.

Historically, dividends of high-quality companies have been known to outgrow inflation, and investors that hold them have always survived periods of high inflation. Because of their ability to increase when price levels are increasing, dividends are an excellent protection against inflation, especially in the long run. For instance, if you hold 2,000 shares of a certain company for $2 a share, which pays an annual dividend of $0.05 per share, you are entitled to collect **$100** in dividend income per annum. If, in the following year, there is 3% inflation, the company increases dividend to $0.1. So, the person receives a dividend of **$200**. The growth in dividends that comes with the right companies helps investors to outpace inflation.

As the years have gone by, the shares of companies that initiate and grow their dividends have done better than the shares of companies that have kept their dividend the same or have not paid dividends at all. **Dividend growth stocks are less sensitive to rising rates as compared to other instruments like bonds.** Looking at history proves that in the United States, dividends have done well during periods of high inflation and even during stagflation. During the key inflation periods of 1940s and the 1970s, there was dividend income growth of over 10%. This shows that dividends are, indeed, a hedge against inflation.

Chapter Quiz/Summary

1. What are a few good investments that can carry you through inflation?
2. Company profits always go down during inflation (True/False)
3. Inflation means that your salary will definitely go up. (True/False)
4. What is the most important way to fight inflation?
5. Company Y is at $20 per share. It pays an annual dividend of $2. If you own 1000 shares, what is your annual dividend income from company Y?

Answers...

1. Gold, Commodities, Real Estate, REITs etc
2. False.
3. False
4. Increased Income
5. $2000 per year

What is Dividend Investing?

Dividend investing is a style of investing where you invest in companies for the main purpose of receiving a passive source of income. You may receive growth in the asset value as well, but the main investing goal is income. This is one of the best ways to invest, considering that most companies that pay dividends are fully grown and very stable. This provides some form of assurance to the investor that the investments will do well. Dividend investing does not usually yield disposable income quickly. In most cases, it requires a long-time horizon for it to fully play out. In the early years of the investment, the dividends received are usually reinvested to compound the income.

Dividend investing is sometimes considered boring by some people. This is because the investment is for slow and steady payments from companies. Steady returns are not boring if you are the investor who understands the essence of long-term investing. Most present-day investors are interested in high yields, unlike the earlier generations of investors who were interested in dividend investing. When investors buy shares in companies, they are paid dividends at the end of a defined period. This may be quarterly, annually, and in some cases, monthly.

What Are Dividends?

Publicly traded companies that generate cash flow and net profit have four ways to deploy the cash. They can invest the money back in the company in the form of research and development. Secondly, they can save the money for a rainy day. They can also buy back shares of the company to support the share price. This is a common American practice known as a stock buyback. And finally, they can pay the money back to shareholders. This payback is known as a dividend. To simplify the understanding of dividends, they can be viewed more like the interest that is earned for keeping money in savings accounts.

The dividend is the amount paid by the company to a shareholder; while the dividend yield is the % yield of the share price paid to the shareholder.

Dividend Yield = (Dividend/Price per share) X 100

The Dividend yield is an indication of your return on investment. For example, if the dividend yield is 5% per year; and you invest $1000; you get $50 per year.

Let's take another example.

For example, if you hold a share whose value is $50, a 5% annual yield will see you earning $2.50 per year per share. The total dividend payout depends on the number and types of shares that you hold.

How Often Are Dividends Paid?

Every company pays dividends at different intervals.

Company dividends are either paid annually (once a year), semi-annually (once every 6 months) or quarterly (once every 3 months).

Who Decides the Dividend Amount?

The Board of Directors of the company decides the dividend to be paid to investors.

What Are Dividend Dates?

Dividend dates for a stock are important dates that all dividend investors need to keep a track of.

There are 4 key dividend dates to keep track of for each dividend payment:

Declaration Date: This is the date on which the board of directors of the company declares the dividend amount.

Ex-Dividend Date: This is the cut-off date for investors to buy the stock to be eligible to receive the dividend. So, investors need to buy the stock before this date to be eligible for the dividend.

Record Date: This is a date when the company makes a list of all shareholders that will receive the dividend on the payment date. So, investors need to buy before the ex-dividend date and sell after the record date to be eligible for the dividend payment.

Payment Date: This is the date when the company pays out the dividend to the shareholders.

Now, let's look at an example of the important dividend dates for company X:

Declaration Date	Ex-Dividend Date	Record Date	Payable Date
June 1st	June 14th	June 15th	July 1st

Company X declares a dividend for its shareholders on June 1st. The company's board of directors then announces a record date of June 15th. Investors who are shareholders on June 15th will be eligible to receive the dividend. Typically, the ex-dividend date would be 1 business day before the record date. In this case it is on June 15th. An investor who purchases shares on or before June 13th and is a shareholder of record on June 15th and will receive the dividend on July 1st.

An investor who purchases shares on or after June 14th will not be entitled to the dividend.

So, the investor who purchases on June 13th or before; and sells on June 16th or after is entitled to the dividend.

Where Can I Get Dividend Information?

Dividendhistory.org is a good spot to get all the dividend information you need. It gives you the ex-dividend date and payment dates of a large number of companies for decades.

You can just search for the company on the search box area on the website:

( )

Search by Symbol or Company

Welcome to DividendHistory.org

Here you'll find dividend information and dividend paying stocks with complete payout histories, increase announcements, growth, yield and much more.

Stock data is currently being added to the database focusing on NYSE, Nasdaq, TSX, LSE and ASX exchanges.

2022-04-21	NDAQ	Nasdaq raises dividend 11% to $0.60 quarterly
2022-04-20	JNJ	Johnson & Johnson raises dividend 6.6% to $1.13 quarterly
2022-04-14	QCOM	QUALCOMM raises dividend 10.3% to $0.75 quarterly
2022-04-14	COST	Costco Wholesale raises dividend 14% to $0.90 quarterly
2022-04-05	PNC	PNC Financial Services raises dividend 20% to $1.50 quarterly
2022-04-04	WSO	Watsco raises dividend 13% to $2.20 quarterly
2022-04-01	TJX	TJX Companies raises dividend 13.6% to $0.295 quarterly
2022-03-31	DOL	Dollarama raises dividend 10% to $0.0553 quarterly
2022-03-30	T	AT&T decreases dividend to $0.2775 due to its upcoming WarnerMedia spinoff
2022-03-25	OXM	Oxford Industries raises dividend 31% to $0.55 quarterly
2023-03-21	MED	Medifast raises dividend 15.5% to $1.64 quarterly

Top Searches (current)

OMC HomeStop

FTS Forts

BEY Best Buy

REI.UN ReUcan RH1

PNC Bank of Nova Scotia

RCI B Rogers Communications

KO Coca-Cola Company

Top Searches (2020)

REI.UN RuCac RUT

AAPL Apple

KHS Enbridge

Types of Dividends

As mentioned in the introduction, there are some companies that offer dividends and others that do not. The main reason for the difference lies with the cash flow. Companies that have stable cash flows usually offer dividends. This is done to raise the confidence of the investors. There are three major types of dividends that can be offered.

Cash

This is the most common dividend type. When a company earns profits, they payout cash as dividends to their investors. These are paid out directly to the investor through their brokerage account. Investors who receive cash dividends in their early years of investing usually reinvest the dividends by buying more shares and growing their portfolios. Only in later years do some investors treat the dividends as disposable income.

Stock

Another name for this is dividend automatic reinvestment. Some companies issue common stocks to shareholders as dividends. The general agreement is usually that when this common stock is issued, it should not exceed 25% of the current shares. If it does, it will be considered to be a stock split. Some investors prefer to receive stock dividends over cash as this helps them to save better. Some find it difficult to reinvest manually, so with stock dividends, the process takes place automatically.

Property

This is another alternative to cash or stock dividends. It is less common than the previous types. In this case, the company issues a tangible asset—products that are sent to shareholders in lieu of cash. Companies that issue dividends are usually those that have a good track record of solid cash flows. The balance sheets of these companies are usually very healthy, and their returns are very high (there are exceptions which we will cover later). There are cases where a company may issue what is known as scrip dividends. This is a promissory note that is issued to the shareholder in the event the company is unable to pay dividends on time.

Investors should know that dividend payments are not always guaranteed. Companies can pay out dividends if they have good cash flows. In times of hardship, these dividends can be cut. When a company cuts its dividends, this is a sign that it is struggling on the financial side. If the dividends continue to be paid on time, it means the company is financially healthy. In most cases, dividends are, therefore, a good measure of the well-being of a company.

Chapter Quiz/Summary

1. Dividends are paid by governments to people (True/False)
2. Dividends are paid by a company to shareholders annually, semi-annually or quarterly (True/False)
3. Dividends are decided by the CEO of the company (True/False).
4. Apple declares a dividend of $0.05 per share to be paid quarterly. If Sam owns 100 shares...
   a. How much dividend income does Sam get per quarter?
   b. How much dividend income does Sam get per year?
5. It's March 5. The Microsoft Board of directors declares a dividend of $2 per share to be paid on April 2nd. All investors who own the stock on March 19th are eligible. The company makes a list of eligible shareholders on March 20th.
   a. What is the announcement date?
   b. What is the ex-dividend date?
   c. What is the record date?
   d. What is the payment date?

Answers:

1. False
2. True
3. False, decided by Board of Directors
4. $5 per quarter; $20 per year
5. March 5th is the announcement date; March 19th is the ex-dividend; March 20th the record date and April 2nd is the payment date.

Getting Started

Dividend investing is one of the best ways to develop a fixed income stream. Many companies pay out dividends, and obviously, some are better than others. You cannot invest in just any dividend stock. Understanding how dividends work is very important. You should know the differences before you jump in. **This chapter will help you to understand how the concept of dividend investing works, and then break down all the steps you need to get started.**

As you know by now, a dividend is a payment that is made to qualified shareholders out of the profits of a company. In most cases, they are paid in the form of cash, although there can be other forms of dividends, as explained in the previous chapter. Dividends are one of the ways that companies offer returns to their shareholders in addition to increasing share prices. The company's board determines the rate at which dividends are paid out and the amounts. This information is readily available before you invest. Sometimes one-off dividend payments are made, for example, if it has been a profitable year.

Step 1: Get a Brokerage Account

You need an online brokerage to trade dividend stocks. It's best to get an international brokerage account so you have access to stocks both in your home country and outside, and you are able to access a wide variety of stocks. Here are the list of brokerages that you can use:

US Brokers

Charles Schwab

Interactive Brokers

FirstTrades

UK Brokers

IG

Interactive Brokers

Australia Brokers

Step 2: Get a List of Dividend Stocks in Your Brokerage Account

Contact your broker or go into the Research section in your online brokerage account and find a list of dividend stocks.

Step 3: Get Dividend Yields for Each Stock

Create an excel sheet that can store relevant data for your research. The first thing you should include for each dividend stock, is the current dividend yield.

Step 4: Get Dividend History for Each Stock

Go to Dividendhistory.com and make a note of the 10-year dividend growth for the stock.

A good place to do this is on dividendhistory.org. It has a good list of dividend stocks all across the world.

Step 5: Get Payout Ratio for Each Stock

Go to finance.yahoo.com and get the payout ratio of the stock. It is located in the Statistics section of the Individual stock in Yahoo finance as shown below for Apple stock:

Search for news, symbols or companies   Sign in   Mail

Finance Home   Watchlists   My Portfolio   Cryptocurrencies   Screeners   Markets   News   Personal Finance   Videos   Yahoo U   ...

Income Statement

Revenue (ttm)	378.32B			
Revenue Per Share (ttm)	22.84	**Dividends & Splits**		
Quarterly Revenue Growth (yoy)	11.20%	Forward Annual Dividend Rate [4]	0.88	
Gross Profit (ttm)	152.84B	Forward Annual Dividend Yield [4]	0.54%	
EBITDA	128.22B	Trailing Annual Dividend Rate [3]	0.87	
Net Income Avi to Common (ttm)	100.55B	Trailing Annual Dividend Yield [3]	0.55%	
Diluted EPS (ttm)	6.01	5 Year Average Dividend Yield [4]	1.11	
Quarterly Earnings Growth (yoy)	20.40%	Payout Ratio [4]	14.34%	
		Dividend Date [2]	Feb 09, 2022	
Balance Sheet		Ex-Dividend Date [4]	Feb 03, 2022	
Total Cash (mrq)	63.91B	Last Split Factor [2]	4:1	
Total Cash Per Share (mrq)	3.92	Last Split Date [3]	Aug 30, 2020	
Total Debt (mrq)	122.8B			
Total Debt/Equity (mrq)	170.71			
Current Ratio (mrq)	1.04			
Book Value Per Share (mrq)	4.40			

Cash Flow Statement

yoy - Year Over Year
lfy - Last Fiscal Year
fye - Fiscal Year Ending

Footnotes

[1] Data provided by Refinitiv
[2] Data provided by EDGAR Online
[3] Data derived from multiple sources or calculated by Yahoo Finance.
[4] Data provided by Morningstar, Inc.
[5] Shares outstanding is taken from the most recently filed quarterly or annual report and Market Cap is calculated using shares outstanding.
[6] Implied Shares Outstanding of common equity, assuming the conversion of all convertible subsidiary equity into common.
[7] EBITDA is calculated by S&P Global Market Intelligence using methodology that may differ from that used by a company in its reporting.
[8] A company's float is a measure of the number of shares available for trading by the public. It's calculated by taking the number of issued and outstanding shares minus any restricted stock, which may not be publicly traded.

Step 6: Get Intrinsic Value for Each Stock

Use the techniques in the next chapter to get the intrinsic value for each stock. Make a note of it in your excel sheet.

Step 7: Get Discount for Each Stock

How far below the intrinsic value is the current value of the stock? Let's say you calculate an intrinsic value of $100 for Microsoft stock (hypothetical situation). If the stock is at $70, the discount rate is 30%.

Step 8: Document all info in an excel sheet for top 10 dividend stocks

Document all the above information for the top 10 stocks that you have picked.

Here's an example below if Microsoft stock was at $160

We like the Dividend history growth of 10% and payout ratio of 20%; but we're not too happy with the Discount and Dividend Yield.

It's only 12.5% below Intrinsic Value. So, if you want to get a margin of safety of 30-50%, you want to wait for the stock to drop more before buying.

Stock Ticker	Dividend Yield (%)	Dividend History (Growth %)	Payout Ratio (%)	Current Value	Intrinsic Value	Discount (%)
MSFT	1.2	10	20	160	140	12.5

Do the same for 9 more stocks.

Step 9: Construct a Diversified Portfolio of Stocks

Use the techniques in Chapter on "Setting Up a Diversified Dividend Portfolio" to ensure that the top 10 stocks represent a properly diversified portfolio.

Buy these stocks when they discounted below intrinsic value. It's preferable to buy stocks at 50% discount; but a 30% discount is acceptable as well.

Also, ensure that they have a low debt to asset value.

I know that these steps could seem a little confusing right now, especially for new investors, but it'll make a whole lot of sense once you go through the different chapters in this book.

Chapter Quiz/Summary

1. The first step to getting started with investing is to get a brokerage account (True / False)
2. What is another name for the real value of a stock?
3. What type of discount below intrinsic value should we buy the stock?
4. How many stocks should be document in the excel sheet?
5. Where should I get the dividend history for the stock?

Answers:

1. True
2. Intrinsic Value
3. 30% or more
4. 20
5. Dividendhistory.org

Dividend Investing for Value Stocks

Dividends are a value investor's best friend. Value investing is a strategy that is employed by investors to discover and validate publicly listed companies before investing in them. The investors do so to find stocks that they believe are undervalued. They compare the share price of the stock to its true value. Value investors thrive on finding and taking advantage of that gap between a stock's intrinsic value and its listed price.

Dividend Investing is a subset of value investing, and we will focus on this subniche in this chapter.

Value Stocks or Growth Stocks?

Growth stocks are the stocks from companies that have the potential to outperform the market in the future. Value stocks are the companies that currently trade below their real value and are expected to appreciate in the future. The major question that most investors have is which one is better: value stocks or growth stocks?

The concept of comparing value stocks and growth stocks generally comes from fundamental stock analysis. Over time, growth stocks are expected to outperform the market. Growth stocks are found in all sectors, that is, small, mid, and large-cap. They keep their growth status until they have achieved their expected potential. These stocks have a very good chance for expansion. The potential comes from the fact that they might have product lines that are expected to sell well in the future. Perhaps they have a competitive advantage that gives them an edge in the market.

Value stocks are those from larger and more established companies that are trading below their actual worth.

There are several reasons for the undervaluing of stocks. In some cases, the price has to do with the general perception of the market. For example, if a company is caught up in a major scandal, people begin to see the company differently and will value it less. This may drive down the stock value. If, however, the company has solid financials, this presents an ideal entry point for investors: the public will eventually forget about what happened with the company and the prices will rise again.

The question is, therefore, which one benefits an investor better. Neither of the two is always correct. Sometimes the stocks may behave adversely. Stocks are usually a blend of these two different categories. This means that they might be undervalued and at the same time have the potential to go above and beyond the current price. When comparing these two factors, it is always important to ascertain the time horizon and the amount of volatility. Value stocks are considered to have a lower risk because they are found in large and established companies. Even if the stock doesn't get to the price that was predicted, they may still offer considerable capital gains.

Growth stocks usually do not pay out dividends directly to the investor. Instead, they reinvest the profits into the company. Growth stocks present a greater probability of loss to the investor, especially if the company cannot keep up with growth expectations. Growth stocks have the highest potential reward, but they come with the highest risk as well. The battle between growth and value stocks has always been complicated. Because of the risks and uncertainty, there cannot be surety over which of the two is the best.

The decision over which stocks to invest in is better left to the investor because it depends on their investment goals and levels of risk tolerance. If the time horizon is a little shorter for both growth and value stocks, their performance will largely depend on the point of the economic cycle that the market is in. If the market is still expanding, the stocks will expand. If it is declining, it is probable that the stocks may also decline. Value stocks tend to outperform during recessions and bear markets, and growth stocks excel in bull markets and economic expansions. Short-term investors and market timers should take this into consideration.

For dividend investing, we prefer value stocks as they are more stable and provide consistent dividends even during times of recession and economic uncertainty.

Why Value Investing?

Value investing is just as easy as described above, but sometimes you need to make careful considerations before you invest in a stock that you perceive to be undervalued.

Value Investing Anchors the Stock Value

The typical value investor studies and goes into minute detail to discover stocks that are being underpriced. Investing in such stocks will see your income increase by a great margin. Dividends are extremely important in value investing, and this is why the company you invest in should have a history of at least 10 years of consistent dividend payments.

They Indicate Quality

It may seem like you are narrowing your scope too much if you insist on something like 10 years of dividend history. However, it is the greatest guarantee you can have because it is impossible to fake 10 years of dividend payments. A smaller number of years is not a very solid foundation. It can be faked.

Sometimes, troubled companies pay out a high dividend for a quarter of two to lure investors in before they go bankrupt. Learn more about this in our chapter on Dividend Investment Traps.

What may eventually happen is not what you expect to happen. You can also look into good corporate governance. Did you know that there are some companies that pay dividends out of borrowed money? The only reason they pay dividends is to safeguard their reputation—a missed dividend could negatively affect their share prices. Be sure that the company's dividends come from profits, not borrowed funds. A good way to check this is to ensure that the company has a low Payout Ratio (<70%); a good Debt to Asset Ratio (<0.5) and a good Debt to Free Cash Flow ratio (<5)

They Contribute Greatly to Your Income

The importance of dividends in an investor's overall return cannot be underestimated. An investor who ignores stocks from dividend-paying companies is not making use of their full earning potential. Dividends offer regular income, and value investing can really be worthwhile. When a stock is undervalued, and you buy it, it may take several years before the market catches up to prove that your perception was correct. This is why I overemphasize the value of patience in dividend investing. The wait is not that difficult, considering that you will be receiving dividend income all the way.

An Extra String to the Bow

Value investing and dividend investing do not need to exist separately. They can go hand in hand. Dividends are very important because they increase returns, and they mitigate risk. Combining dividend investing and value investing will help you to do better with your investing.

Determining the Intrinsic Value of a Stock

Every asset has some sort of intrinsic value that is not influenced by external factors. In most cases there are external factors that influence the value of stocks. There can be other factors like unemployment, politics, inflation, and Gross Domestic Product (GDP) figures. When determining the intrinsic value of a stock, boil down the external factors so that you come up with the value of a stock based on its own merits. The intrinsic value is influenced by internal factors like the quality of management of a firm, the products, the brand strength, and the market strength.

When it comes to stock market investing, investors are interested in the cash that is available to stockholders. The internal factors listed here are a determinant of the cash that a company is likely to generate. There are methods that are used in calculating the intrinsic worth of a stock on the basis of the cash generated as well as the expectations for growth in the future.

One of the main reasons why investors are interested in intrinsic value is because it helps them to spot stocks that are underpriced. When a stock is priced lower than its calculated intrinsic value, it means the current market price is a bargain and a good investment. The different methods of calculating the intrinsic value are the price to book value, dividend discount method and the discounted cash flow method.

Method 1: Using the Price to Book Value

There are some key things that you can look out for in a company's balance sheet. These things will help you to determine the intrinsic value of a company. It is very important to know what the company can earn from the assets that are on the balance sheet. The term "balance sheet" describes a document that reflects the assets, liabilities, and equity of a company. It shows the assets that the company owns and how it is financed, that is, debt and liabilities.

The book value is an important indicator of a company's current valuation, that is based on formula below:

Book Value per Share = Equity / Number of Shares

Equity is also known as the value or the shareholders' equity. If you divide the equity by the number of outstanding shares, you will come up with the book price per share.

Price to book value is calculated using the formula below:

Price to Book Value = Price per Share/Book Value per Share

Now, let's look at an example...

Consider the following information for ABC company:

	2014	2015
Equity	210,185.00	221,857.00
Common Stock Outstanding Numbers	3083.037	3099.48

ABC's book value (2014)   = 210,185/3083.037

= 68.174

ABC'S Book Value (2015) = 221,857/3099.48

= 71.57

If the price of ABC in March 2016 was \$42.83, then we calculate the price to book value based on 2014/2015 book value below (as we do not have equity information for 2016 till the end of the year):

2014:   \$42.83/68.174 = 0.6268x

2015: $42.83/71.57 = 0.5983$x

A low price to book value, especially below 1, is often a signal to investors that a stock is undervalued. If it is greater than 1, the best possible interpretation is that the stock is trading at a premium.

There is some risk on the rate of return on investment, as anything can happen in the global economy. So, we want to add a factor of safety of 50%.

So, we want to see a book value of below 0.5 before we invest, to account for the 50% Margin of Safety.

Let's look at a second example. Let's look at Amazon stock. It's trading at $2485.93 in 2022, as shown on Yahoo Finance below.

Amazon.com, Inc. (AMZN)
NasdaqGS - NasdaqGS Real-time price. Currency in USD

2,485.63 406.30 (-14.05%) **2,478.75** -6.88 (-0.28%)
At Close: 04:00PM EDT   After hours: 07:59PM EDT

| Summary | Chart | Statistics | Historical data | Profile | Financials | Analysis | Options | Holders | Sustainability |

Previous close	2,891.93	Market cap	1.471T
Open	2,596.98	Beta (5Y monthly)	1.12
Bid	2,474.98 x 1300	PE ratio (TTM)	38.35
Ask	2,475.90 x 1100	EPS (TTM)	64.81
Day's range	2,432.78 - 2,615.22	Earnings date	27 July 2022 - 01 Aug 2022
52-week range	2,432.50 - 3,773.08	Forward dividend & yield	N/A (N/A)
Volume	13,479,948	Ex-dividend date	N/A
Avg. volume	3,857,733	1y target est	4,032.39

Let's have a look at last year's equity. We go to the Financials tab
and look at Balance sheet to get the Equity and Number of shares.

Amazon.com, Inc. (AMZN)
NasdaqGS - NasdaqGS Real-time price. Currency in USD

2,485.63 -406.30 (-14.05%) **2,478.75** -6.88 (-0.28%)
At close: 04:00PM EDT   After hours: 07:59PM EDT

| Summary | Chart | Statistics | Historical data | Profile | Financials | Analysis | Options | Holders | Sustainability |

Show: Income statement   Balance sheet   Cash flow   Annual   Quarterly

Balance sheet   All numbers in thousands

Breakdown	30/12/2021	30/12/2020	30/12/2019	30/12/2018
⌄ Assets				

Accounts payable	78,664,000	72,539,000	47,183,000	38,192,000
Accrued liabilities	51,775,000	44,138,000	32,439,000	23,663,000
Deferred revenues	11,827,000	9,708,000	8,190,000	6,536,000
Total current liabilities	142,266,000	126,385,000	87,812,000	68,391,000
⌄ Non-current liabilities				
Long-term debt	48,744,000	31,816,000	23,414,000	23,495,000
Deferred tax liabilities	-	-	-	2,386,000
Other long-term liabilities	23,643,000	17,017,000	12,171,000	8,535,000
Total non-current liabilities	140,038,000	101,406,000	75,376,000	50,708,000
Total liabilities	282,304,000	227,791,000	163,188,000	119,099,000
⌄ Stockholders' equity				
Common stock	5,000	5,000	5,000	5,000
Retained earnings	85,915,000	52,551,000	31,220,000	19,625,000
Accumulated other comprehe...	-1,376,000	-180,000	-986,000	-1,035,000
Total stockholders' equity	138,245,000	93,404,000	62,060,000	43,549,000
Total liabilities and stockholde...	420,549,000	321,195,000	225,248,000	162,648,000

So, Amazon Equity = 138,245,000*1000 = 138000 million = 138 billion

We can find the number of shares in the Statistics tab of Yahoo Finance.

Amazon.com, Inc. (AMZN)
NasdaqGS - NasdaqGS Real-time price. Currency in USD

2,485.63 -406.30 (-14.05%)   **2,478.75** -6.88 (-0.28%)
At close: 04:00PM EDT   After hours: 07:59PM EDT

Summary   Chart   **Statistics**   Historical data   Profile   Financials   Analysis   Options   Holders   Sustainabil

Valuation measures[4]   **Trading information**

Valuation measures[4]		Trading information	
Market cap (intra-day)	1.47T	**Stock price history**	
Enterprise value	1.49T	Beta (5Y monthly)	1.12
Trailing P/E	44.55	52-week change [3]	-26.60%
Forward P/E	52.63	S&P500 52-week change [3]	-1.45%
PEG ratio (5-yr expected)	2.72	52-week high [3]	3,773.08
Price/sales (ttm)	3.16	52-week low [3]	2,432.50
Price/book (mrq)	10.62	50-day moving average [3]	3,054.25
Enterprise value/revenue	3.17	200-day moving average [3]	3,277.53
Enterprise value/EBITDA	20.05		
		Share statistics	
Financial highlights		Avg vol (3-month) [3]	3.86M
		Avg vol (10-day) [3]	4.49M
Fiscal year		Shares outstanding [5]	508.54M
Fiscal year ends	30 Dec 2021	Implied shares outstanding [6]	N/A
Most-recent quarter (mrq)	30 Dec 2021	Float [8]	457.99M

Amazon Shares Outstanding = 508.54 million

Amazon Book Value (2021) = \$138000 / 508.54 = \$2710

Amazon Current Share Price = \$2485.63

Book Value Per Share = $2485.63/$2710 = 0.92

If you want a 50% Margin of Safety, you want to wait till the Book value per share hits 0.5.

Method 2: The Discounted Cash Flow Method

This is the most widely used method of calculating the intrinsic value and it is often referred to as the DCF method. To come up with value, this method uses free cash flows in place of dividends. This is a very flexible method because it takes into account the variations in cash flows from year to year. The method is also applicable to any company regardless of size. In calculating the intrinsic value, here are the steps to be followed.

- Make a projection of the free cash flows during the forecast years. Put down how much you expect the cash flows to grow over the forecast period.

- Determine a discount rate. Focus on the assumed cost of equity or the growth rate of the company. The estimate can, for example, be something like 8%.

- Discount the cash flows that you have projected to their present value.

$$DCF = \frac{CF_1}{(1+r)^1} + \frac{CF_2}{(1+r)^2} + \cdots \cdots \cdots \frac{CF_n}{(1+r)^n}$$

DCF = Present Discounted Cash flow

CF_i = Cash flow for future year i

r = Expected rate of growth in cash flow

n = The last year of Expected cash flow

The above formula, from Corporate Finance, may seem complicated, but it can be easily explained with an example.

Stock ABC is priced at $25. The stock is expected to generate income over the next five years. In the first two years, it is expected to generate a cash flow of $8, and in the third year, $14. It is also expected to generate $28 in the fourth year and $90 in the fifth year. Suppose the expected growth rate of the cash is 7%, then calculating the DCF is done as shown below:

$$DCF = \$8/(1+7\%)^1 + \$8/(1+7\%)^2 + \$14/(1+7\%)^3 + \$28/(1+7\%)^4 + \$90/(1+7\%)^5$$

$$DCF = \$8/(1.07)^1 + \$8/(1.07)^2 + \$14/(1.07)^3 + \$28/(1.07)^4 + \$90/(1.07)^5$$

$$DCF = \mathbf{\$19.94}$$

During the five-year period, $148 cash flow would be generated by the company. However, when you discount the cash flow to the present value it is only $19.94.

$19.94 is the intrinsic value of the cash flows done by the company.

So, the company is considered overvalued unless it falls below $19.

So, it is not a good idea to buy the company at a price of $25.

I would personally not buy this stock unless it falls below $9.50 (50% discount).

Method 3: The Dividend Discount Method

Better known as the DDM, the dividend discount method is a quick and easy method to determine the intrinsic value of a stock. It is mostly used by large, stable companies. This method utilizes a formula that is based on dividends, giving much consideration to their value in the present as well as projected growth as time progresses (Alvarez, 2022). The formula is as follows:

Intrinsic stock price = $DPS_1/(r-g)$, where:

DPS_1 = Expected dividends in a year

r = the discount rate or simply the expected rate of return on investment

g = the growth rate of dividends per annum in perpetuity

For instance, a company that has a large and stable customer base may expect to pay $20 on every share in a year when there has been a stable 4% growth rate. This means that the g in the formula is 4%. If the required rate of return is 8%, it represents the r in the formula. The calculation of the intrinsic value of the share would look like this:

Intrinsic price = $20/ (.08-.04) =**$500**

So, we invest in the company if it is at or below $250 (50% Margin of Safety) based on the dividend discount method.

Dividend Discount Model

The Dividend Discount model can be calculated using two different methods.

Zero Discount Model

The zero-discount model formula assumes a zero growth rate for the company stock price. It is as follows:

P_0 = **Div/r** where:

P_0 = price at time zero, with no dividend growth

Div = future dividend payments

r = discount rate / expected growth rate

This model works if there is no assumption of company growth. For example, for a company that has a required rate of return of 9% and pays dividends of $1.50 per year, the intrinsic value is calculated as follows:

Intrinsic value = Annual Dividend/Expected Rate of Return

=$1.50/0.09

=$16.66

So, after considering factor of safety, I would invest if it was below $8.33

Constant Dividend Growth Model

If a stock is paying a $6 dividend, with a steady growth of 8% per year, and assuming that the expected rate of return is **10%**:

Intrinsic Value =D*((1+g)/(r-g))

where D is the dividend; r the growth rate and g is the growth rate

$$= 6\,(1+0.08)/(0.10-0.08)$$

Intrinsic Value   = **$324.00**

So, after taking into account factor of safety, I would invest if it was below $162.

Which Method to Use?

Using any of these methods, you can come up with the intrinsic value of stocks. I am sure by now you have realized that to calculate the intrinsic value of a smaller company, the discounted cash flows are more ideal.

For larger and stable companies, which are not subject to as much volatility, the dividend discount method is ideal. Besides, you cannot use the dividend discount method on a company that does not even pay dividends.

The simplest method to calculate the intrinsic value is the **Price to Book Value** method, and this is the method I recommend for beginners.

For those who have the ability and patience, I recommend using **all the methods,** and then using the lowest intrinsic value found as your base value. This gives you the maximum possible margin of safety. Buying quality stocks at 50% margin of safety gives you a huge advantage.

A Short message from the Author:

Hey, are you enjoying the book? I'd love to hear your thoughts!

Many readers do not know how hard reviews are to come by, and how much they help an author.

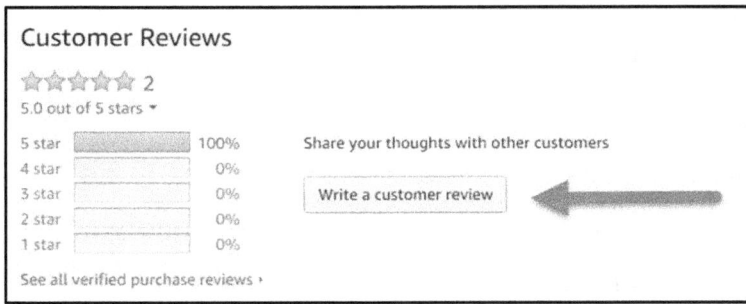

I would be incredibly thankful if you could take just 60 seconds to write a brief review on Amazon, even if it's just a few sentences!

Thank you for taking the time to share your thoughts!

Your review will genuinely make a difference for me and help gain exposure for my work.

Dividend Investing for Commodity Stocks

Commodity stocks are stocks that are backed by valuable resources that are essential. Investing in commodity stocks gives you a certain level of confidence, since they have daily consumption characteristics. One example is stocks that are issued by steel companies. There may be great fluctuations in the price of iron ore or copper, but the risk of it becoming obsolete is very low. The general implication is that there is always some value in commodity stocks, and this provides a margin of guarantee that investors want.

Commodity stocks, at most times, issue dividends to investors. This is good for investors because, besides enjoying the safety of commodity stocks, they also get regular income payments from them. The main reason why investors love commodity stocks is because of the dividend payments which are guaranteed. The fluctuation in the price of the stock does not really matter to the investors. The strategy of investing in commodity stocks is solid because it does not depend on stock market appreciation for its success.

Why do Commodity Stocks Have High Dividends?

Investments in commodity stocks are growing very fast. As explained above, there are advantages that investors love, and this is why the sector is growing rapidly. One of the reasons why investors love these stocks is because the dividends are almost always high. Here are some of the reasons why commodity stocks yield high dividends.

Minimal Outside Influences

The stock market in general is often bombarded by several outside influences. This is not the case with commodity stocks. They have this unreal security against external factors. This is because when investing in commodity stocks, you are not just investing in a piece of a company that is co-owned by a few individuals. The fact is that you are investing in the physical products and raw materials that are needed for everyday survival. It is unlikely that the commodity prices completely sink to zero. Some of the commodities that usually back commodity stocks include natural gas, minerals like silver and copper, sugar, and coffee. These commodities have designated exchanges that they trade on throughout the United States. Most of these exchanges are found in New York, London and Chicago.

Commodity Price Changes Are Predictable

Upward or downward price movements in commodity stocks is easier to predict and are quite methodical. This is because investors are better able to get a handle on the movements since there are not as many sources of commodity data that may give out conflicting facts. Of late, there have been large hedge funds that have invested in commodities, but these do not have much of a directional impact on the behavior of the stocks. There may be resultant upward movements, but they are temporary; the commodity markets are so large that they do not take much time to get back to themselves again.

Because commodity markets are large, they are able to accommodate different players with their diversities without much of a hitch. The chart analysis, inventory, and growing cycle data in the commodities market make way for more predictable movements. This is very important for investors because there are not as many surprises in the market. They almost always know what follows and what to expect in the coming months. Wouldn't we say that knowledge brings a lot of peace of mind? The dividends are not very much affected at any time because of this.

Commodities Offer a Better Tax Break Due to Dividend

Commodities often receive favorable tax treatment in the US, as compared to stocks and stock options. Most investors operate on a short-term basis that could span less than a year. The short-term gains on commodities and commodity options are usually split on a 60/40 basis. This implies that 60% of the short-term gains are taxed at the lower, long-term rate, and 40% of the gains are taxed higher. It is always advisable that before jumping headlong into commodities, you consult with a tax professional to be sure of your options; as tax options will differ based on region.

For the reasons listed and explained here, commodity stocks often pay high dividends to investors. They have turned out to be a lifesaver in the investment world because they make investing so much easier. Commodity investing can be viewed as ideal for new investors who may not yet have mastered the art of predicting market behavior.

Commodity Cycles

What are Commodity Cycles? How do they work?

It is very important for investors who buy in commodity stocks to understand the commodity cycle. The cycle is important because it helps investors to determine future direction. Every commodity goes through the commodity cycle, which is mostly driven by the investment behavior of producers.

A commodity cycle usually begins with a huge increase in prices of the commodity due to undersupply. This leads to a commodity boom, and a lot of producers start getting into the market.

The producers compete, leading to oversupply and a crash in commodity prices. Other factors like recessions lead to an even lower demand in oil supply and leads to lower prices. This leads to a lot of businesses going bust; and producers are hesitant to start more supply.

Over time, this leads to another period of undersupply, and the cycle repeats.

If you intend to invest in commodities successfully, you should be able to identify where a commodity is relative to its cycle. It would be ideal to get in at the start and go along with the cycle.

Let's look at a 20-year price chart of oil. Commodity price history charts are found easily at Macrotrends.com and you can easily zoom into any period of time. Make sure that you remove the log scale and set it to Inflation-Adjusted values. Now, let's have a look at the oil commodity chart.

Link: https://www.macrotrends.net/1369/crude-oil-price-history-chart

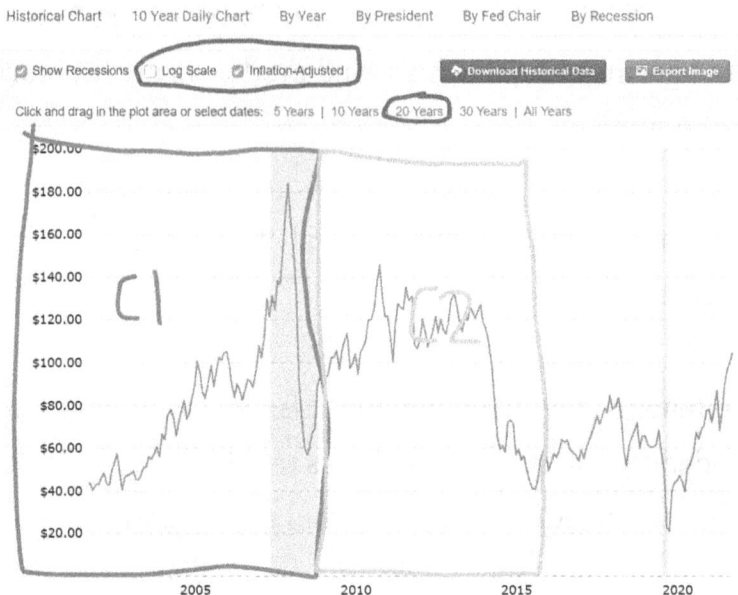

You see the part that is highlighted in red is an oil cycle between 2000-2008. Oil prices started increasing in 2000. Between 2000-2008 there was a was a decreasing supply of oil, which led to an increase in prices. In 2006-2008, there was a huge increase in oil producers looking to take advantage of high oil prices. There was also a decrease in demand from the Great Recession.

This led to a huge crash in the price of oil in 2008.

That was the point when a lot of oil producers went out of business.

And then, we had a similar cycle play out between 2008-2015.

So, we recommend buying high quality, high dividend stocks when oil is below **$60 per barrel (inflation-adjusted price)**, as seen in chart below.

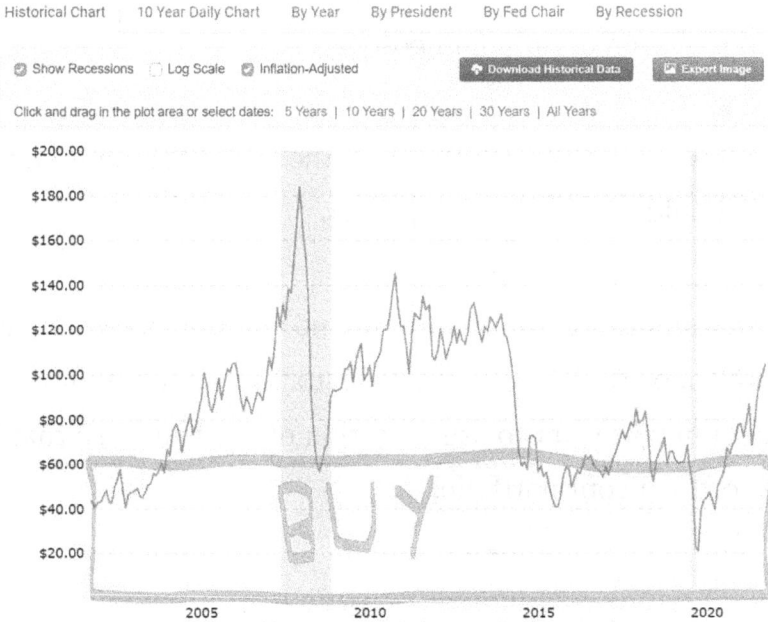

Keep reinvesting the dividends till you reach the other end of the oil cycle, and then you can start taking profits.

All commodities, whether it be copper, iron, wheat, corn, have a cycle that is based on the supply demand curve. You can find these charts at Macrotrends. Make sure you look at inflation adjusted returns over 50 years, and start buying high dividend, high quality stocks at the bottom of the commodity cycle.

If you own the stock and the stock is at the top of the commodity chart, you should consider taking profits.

Remember, you want to make sure that no stock is more than 5% of your portfolio. So, if you bought oil stocks in 2009 and it has doubled; you might want to sell a portion of your stock so that it gets back to 5% of your portfolio,

How to Choose Commodity Stocks

Step 1: Choose your commodity

Use the commodity cycle charts as described above to pick the best commodity for your portfolio.

Step 2: Get a List of 10 Large Cap Commodity Stocks

Start looking through your brokerage for global commodity stocks. It's important for your brokerage to be able to trade globally. A lot of the best commodity stocks are outside the United States. Your brokerage should have a research section to pick out top quality commodity stocks. If you cannot find the section, call your brokerage to find out. Make sure that that you pick 20 large cap stocks. These stocks have a market cap of at least 10 billion. These stocks are more stable, and more likely to pay dividends.

Step 3: Filter out high debt companies

You want to filter out companies that have a lot of debt. The debt to asset ratio should be less than 0.5. We will show you an example of how to do this in the next section.

Step 4: Check the dividend history

Check the dividend history of the stocks in dividendhistory.org. Make sure you check that the company does not cut dividend payment during down cycles for the commodity. Filter out any companies that don't have a consistent dividend history.

Step 6: Check the payout ratio

The payout ratio tells you what percentage of the company's profits are used to pay out dividends. If a company is paying out too much of its profits to pay dividends, it is very unhealthy and could be a dividend trap. We want to invest in companies with payout ratios below 50%. Filter out companies with payout ratios above 50%.

We will show you an example of how to do this in the next section.

Step 6: Buy the high dividend companies

Buy the top 5 companies by dividend yield. Make sure that no single stock is more than 5% of your portfolio.

Debt – Asset Ratio

The debt to Asset Ratio is a good indicator of the financial health of a commodity producer. Cash flows may not be a good indicator as these go up and down with the commodity cycle. A company with a high debt to asset ratio will have lower dividend yields and is more likely to go bankrupt during a down cycle.

So, how do we check this? We look at Yahoo Finance Balance sheet tab under Financials.

Let's look at the example of Chevron.

Chevron Corporation (CVX)
NYSE - NYSE Delayed Price. Currency in USD

156.67 -5.12 (-3.16%) **157.25** +0.58 (+0.37%)
At close: April 29 04:02PM EDT   After hours: Apr 29, 07:59PM EDT

Summary   Chart   Conversations   Statistics   Historical Data   Profile   **Financials**   Analysis   Options   Holders   Sustainability

Show: Income Statement   **Balance Sheet**   Cash Flow   Annual   Quarterly

Breakdown	12/30/2021	12/30/2020	12/30/2019	12/30/2018
> Total Assets	239,535,000	239,790,000	237,428,000	253,863,000
> Total Liabilities Net Minority Int...	99,595,000	107,064,000	92,220,000	98,221,000
⌄ Total Equity Gross Minority Inte...	139,940,000	132,726,000	145,208,000	155,642,000
> Stockholders' Equity	139,067,000	131,688,000	144,213,000	154,554,000
Minority Interest	873,000	1,038,000	995,000	1,088,000
Total Capitalization	169,731,000	174,008,000	167,622,000	183,287,000
Common Stock Equity	139,067,000	131,688,000	144,213,000	154,554,000
Capital Lease Obligations	449,000	447,000	282,000	.
Net Tangible Assets	134,682,000	127,286,000	139,750,000	150,036,000
Working Capital	6,947,000	3,895,000	1,799,000	6,850,000
Invested Capital	169,987,000	175,556,000	170,904,000	189,013,000
Tangible Book Value	134,682,000	127,286,000	139,750,000	150,036,000
Total Debt	31,369,000	44,315,000	26,973,000	34,459,000
Net Debt	25,280,000	38,272,000	21,005,000	25,117,000
Share Issued	2,442,677	2,442,677	2,442,677	2,442,677
Ordinary Shares Number	1,929,806	1,925,186	1,882,168	1,902,838
Treasury Shares Number	512,871	517,490	560,508	539,839

It has a debt of 31,369,000 and total assets of 239,535,000. So, it has a debt to asset ratio of **0.13**, which is amazing. We like all stocks with a debt to asset ratio below 0.5.

Now, let's look at the payout ratio. It's under Yahoo Finance Statistics tab.

Return on Assets (ttm)	4.14%	Short % of Float (Apr 13, 2022) [4]	1.19%
Return on Equity (ttm)	11.51%	Short % of Shares Outstanding (Apr 13, 2022) [4]	1.19%
		Shares Short (prior month Mar 14, 2022) [4]	32.02M
Income Statement			
Revenue (ttm)	155.61B	**Dividends & Splits**	
Revenue Per Share (ttm)	81.21	Forward Annual Dividend Rate [4]	5.68
Quarterly Revenue Growth (yoy)	84.60%	Forward Annual Dividend Yield [4]	3.63%
Gross Profit (ttm)	66.23B	Trailing Annual Dividend Rate [3]	5.31
EBITDA	33.4B	Trailing Annual Dividend Yield [3]	3.28%
Net Income Avi to Common (ttm)	15.62B	5 Year Average Dividend Yield [4]	4.47
Diluted EPS (ttm)	8.14	Payout Ratio [4]	65.23%
Quarterly Earnings Growth (yoy)	N/A	Dividend Date [3]	Mar 09, 2022
		Ex-Dividend Date [4]	Feb 14, 2022
Balance Sheet			
Total Cash (mrq)	5.67B	Last Split Factor [2]	2:1
Total Cash Per Share (mrq)	2.91	Last Split Date [3]	Sep 12, 2004

We see that Chevron has a payout ratio of **65.23%**, which is acceptable. We prefer payout ratios below 50%, so we would wait for Chevron to get a better payout ratio.

Chapter Quiz/Summary

1. What is the most important part about choosing a commodity to trade?
2. A commodity stock has a debt to asset ratio of 1.3 with a high dividend. Should we buy this stock?
3. A commodity stock has a payout ratio of 90% with a high dividend. Should we buy this stock?
4. How large should a commodity dividend stock market cap be?
5. At what part of the commodity cycle should we buy?

Answers:

1. The commodity cycle.
2. No, it has too much debt. It should be below 0.5
3. No, the dividend is unsustainable. The payout ratio should be below 70%.
4. 10 billion or more
5. At the bottom of the commodity cycle.

Dividend Growth Investing

There is nothing that excites people more than earning income while sitting at the beach. This is what companies discovered a long time ago when dividends were first created; dividends are the investor's path to passive income. When an investor holds enough stocks that pay dividends, they receive a regular paycheck through the dividends. This is fantastic for many investors. But for it to come to fruition, you must invest a substantial amount of money. You cannot expect much out of a small investment.

The dividend growth strategy works if you have a lot of money invested in companies that have hefty growing dividend yields. This helps you to earn the most out of your investment. This may sound easy, but you must never forget that your investment can be affected adversely, which may see you lose your money. This is exactly what happened to investors who had invested their money right before the COVID-19 pandemic. They found themselves losing more than 30% of their earnings. The pandemic caused multiple stocks to plunge. Some stocks did so by more than 85%. Millions of dollars were lost.

The general idea behind avoiding losing your money is to choose high quality stocks. When you find good stocks, you must be informed about what to do with them, and at the same time, you should know the pitfalls to avoid. Many investors have fallen into an expensive pit, making it difficult for them to ever rise again. Many investors are blinded by their love for passive income. This is why this section has been specifically designed to help you to understand how to invest in dividend growth stocks and how to stay afloat while doing so.

What are Dividend Growth Stocks?

Dividend growth stocks are those stocks that have **a consistent record of increasing their dividends over time**. But unlike other dividend stocks, they also invest a part of their cash flow into growth and expansion of their company.

Dividend growth not only consistently increase their dividends; they also increase their stock value, cash flows and equity at a consistent value.

With the dividend growth investing strategy, the investor chooses and invests in stocks that have a growing dividend yield. The investor is actively involved in the market to identify such stocks and invest in them. The main reason why investors employ this strategy is to maximize their chances of earning passive income. Dividend growth investing is considered to be more stable than other forms of investment. Investors from different walks of life flock to this strategy because it works in almost any sector. Many people place their savings—for example, retirement savings—into dividend growth stocks. This is done in an attempt to grow their earnings significantly.

How Does the Strategy Work?

Put simply, dividend growth investing is quite easy when compared to other forms of investing. The investor must make selections of stocks that pay investors high dividends and place their money in them. The best stocks to go for are those that have a long-standing track record of having paid dividends to investors.

There is, however, more to this strategy than there is on paper. There are several aspects to be considered before investing using this strategy. For example, you must probe into the quality of the dividends that have been paid to investors over the years. Consistent growth for several years is more favorable than growth over one or two years followed by much lower growth. Consistency in quality is key.

Once an investor has selected stocks and begun to invest, the dividends should then start to come in. It is up to the investor to figure out what to do with their dividends. They can live off them or spend them in any way they might please. However, for dividend growth investing to fully work, there is a need to reinvest the dividends to set up higher earnings. When you reinvest, the next time the dividends come in, they will be higher, and so on when you reinvest yet again. The cycle continues.

As a dividend investor, you must ensure that your portfolio grows over time. To some investors, it may sound too good to be true. Of course, there are risks involved when it comes to dividend growth investing, and the investor should be aware of them. Try to educate yourself as much as possible about dividend growth investing, so that when you set up your investment, you factor in every possible factor. The health of your investments depends on how carefully set up your portfolio is.

How to Spot Quality Growth Stocks?

Finding the best company to invest in is critical when it comes to dividend growth investing. It is important to select companies that have been paying high dividends for a long time, but there is more to the selection process than that. There are other aspects of the company that you must look into. All these aspects, put together, add up to quality growth stocks. So, you should remember that it is not only dividends that you should look for, but there are also other important factors to be considered, which include consistent cash flows, company size, and potential for growth.

Ex-Dividend Date	Payout Date	Cash Amount	% Change
2011-08-16	2011-09-08	$0.16	
2011-05-17	2011-06-09	$0.16	
2011-02-15	2011-03-10	$0.16	
2010-11-16	2010-12-09	$0.16	↑ 23.08%
2010-08-17	2010-09-09	$0.13	
2010-05-18	2010-06-10	$0.13	
2010-02-16	2010-03-11	$0.13	
2009-11-17	2009-12-10	$0.13	
2009-08-18	2009-09-10	$0.13	
2009-05-19	2009-06-18	$0.13	
2009-02-17	2009-03-12	$0.13	
2008-11-18	2008-12-11	$0.13	↑ 18.18%
2008-08-19	2008-09-11	$0.11	
2008-05-13	2008-06-12	$0.11	
2008-02-19	2008-03-13	$0.11	

Previous Next

Above is a dividend history chart of Microsoft (MSFT). Here you see that the dividends paid during the 2007-2008 recession. Not only were the dividends paid during this period, but they also actually increased by 18%. This is an indicator of a strong recession proof dividend stock.

Another company, Ford cut its dividend during the 2008 and 2020 recessions temporarily. Thus, Microsoft is a better dividend growth company than Ford; even though Ford offers high dividends.

Many companies know that many investors only look at dividends and can easily be fooled. For this reason, companies engage in practices that deceive investors. Did you know that borrowed money can be used to pay dividends and maintain consistency when in fact the company is not doing well? Therefore, it is vital to make a close analysis of the performance of the company to be sure of its actual position. Here are some points to note in spotting good dividend growth stocks.

The Divided Yields Must Be Much Higher than Bank Interest Rates; and Preferably Beat Inflation

The dividend yields out of the investment must be significant. If you look at the dividend yield plus annual growth rate without factoring in inflation, you may think that you are making money, yet you are not. You should therefore ensure that when you invest, the dividends are above the inflation rate to allow for accumulation and growth. Specifically searching for stocks that beat the inflation rate is very difficult because the rates of inflation change on a constant basis. However, this consideration still has to be made time and again.

The Company Should Have Low Debt

The only reason companies with debt may offer high dividends is because they want to encourage investors to invest their money to boost cash flows. This is quite worrying because the payment of dividends by the company is dependent on debt and sales. It is only a matter of time before schemes like those fall apart and the investors lose out. Things may turn sour if the company does not get as many investors as may have been expected. An ideal stock to invest in is one that has a debt-to-equity ratio of 0.5 or lower; preferably below 0.3.

Now, let's have a look at an example of a company with a good and bad debt profile.

Let's look at AMC stock on Yahoo Finance Statistics tab.

AMC Entertainment Holdings, Inc. (AMC)
NYSE - NYSE Delayed Price. Currency in USD

☆ Add to watchlist

15.30 -0.34 (-2.17%) **15.32** +0.02 (+0.13%)
At close: April 29 04:00PM EDT   After hours: Apr 29. 07:59PM EDT

Advertisement

Summary   Chart   Conversations   Statistics   Historical Data   Profile   Financials   Analysis   Options   Holders   Sustainability

Advertisement

Show: Income Statement   Balance Sheet   Cash Flow   Annual   Quarterly

Balance Sheet   All numbers in thousands   ↙ Expand All

Balance Sheet All numbers in thousands

Breakdown	12/30/2021	12/30/2020	12/30/2019	12/30/2018
> Total Assets	10,821,500	10,276,400	13,675,800	9,495,800
> Total Liabilities Net Minority Int...	12,611,000	13,134,600	12,461,600	8,097,800
> Total Equity Gross Minority Inte...	-1,789,500	-2,858,200	1,214,200	1,398,000
Total Capitalization	3,618,500	2,810,700	5,947,600	6,105,800
Common Stock Equity	-1,789,500	-2,885,100	1,214,200	1,398,000
Capital Lease Obligations	5,323,400	5,667,600	5,599,500	669,800
Net Tangible Assets	-4,372,700	-5,595,600	-3,770,200	-3,742,800
Working Capital	82,400	-1,091,500	-1,260,100	-546,800
Invested Capital	3,638,500	2,830,700	5,967,600	6,188,000
Tangible Book Value	-4,372,700	-5,595,600	-3,770,200	-3,742,800
Total Debt	10,751,400	11,383,400	10,352,900	5,459,800
Net Debt	3,835,500	5,407,500	4,488,400	4,476,700
Share Issued	513,979	228,066	107,582	107,208
Ordinary Shares Number	513,979	224,333	103,850	103,475
Treasury Shares Number	-	3,733	3,733	3,733

It has a total debt of 10,751,400 and total assets of 10,821,500. So, the debt to asset ratio is 0.99 (10,751,400/10,821,500). So, AMC is a company we want to avoid investing in as it has a debt to asset ratio way above 0.5.

Now, let's look at Apple stock (AAPL).

From Yahoo finance again, it has a debt of 124,719,000 and total assets of 351,002,000. The debt to asset ratio is 0.36. This is within our acceptable range of 0-0.5. So, we consider Apple to be in a good financial position.

The Company Should Have Enough Cash on Hand

Companies with cash on hand are good to invest in. Sometimes a company may not have debt but may still be unable to pay dividends that are as high as you might expect. Most companies make dividend promises out of the revenue that they are currently earning. Imagine what would happen if that revenue fell. The company would be forced to borrow or to employ strategies that allow it to sell more shares in order to pay dividends. As long as a company borrows money to keep its investors happy, it is not operating on the healthy side. Cash on hand is an indication that the company can honor its obligations and still have money to spare. This implies that the stocks of such a company are good, and growth can be guaranteed.

The cash ratio is a good way to measure the strength of a company's cash position.

Cash ratio is measured as:

Cash ratio = Cash available/Total liabilities

We want the company to have a cash ratio of 0.5 or above; ideally above 1.

Now, let's have a look at Apple's cash ratio. Apple has an available cash of 63.91 billion and total liabilities of 28.79 billion. Apple has a cash ratio of 2.21, which is incredibly good.

Companies With Long Term Growth Expectations

Continuity in the growth of a company is something you should look for. A company may have done well in the several years that you review, but things may turn for the worse and it may not perform as well anymore. There are cases where, because of technological advancements, some companies that used to do well are being forced out of business. The expectation should be that the company will continue to grow in the foreseeable future. This may be difficult to ascertain but, at the least, most factors should be pointing toward that. If a company does not look like it will grow in the long term, investing in it may not be a very good idea.

Over the years, companies whose stocks grow consistently have outperformed the market. Dividend growth stocks do that well. It is true that, by steering away from low-growth stocks, you will be doing yourself a great favor. Stocks that pay growing dividends have also outperformed those that do not. Dividend growth investing has become the order of the day. This is not a bad thing because, if the dividends don't grow, your earnings will be stunted.

The Power of the Dividend Snowball

A dividend snowball refers to a progressive cycle where dividend income continues to grow, mainly as the result of a dividend reinvestment strategies. To kickstart the dividend snowball, you should make an investment in high quality **dividend growth stock** shares. Your investment will generate income and, to increase it, you should continue to add more funds either by reinvesting dividends or adding an investment. The more you do this, the more you earn from your investments. The earnings that started small will begin to grow, which is why it is referred to as the dividend snowball. This chapter will help you to create your own dividend snowball. Let's get started!

Regularly Inject Money into Your Investments

As is often said, it takes money to make more money. The biggest financial task that you may be faced with is to make more money. You can increase your chances of making more money to inject into your investments by improving your skills, creating more value in your business, and working hard at a side hustle that generates more income for you. Having earned the money, you should be able to save more for the creation of your snowball. You can ensure this by cutting down on your spending and having more leftover income.

Reinvest All the Dividends That You Receive

When you receive dividends, you can choose to invest them again to increase your future dividends. There are two options for the reinvestments process.

Automatic Dividend Reinvestment

Reinvesting can be automated through your brokerage firm and reinvest the dividends paid by buying more shares in the same company. The advantage of this option is that once you set things up, you can forget about reinvesting and just watch your portfolio grow. What you do when reinvesting automatically is that you give a standing instruction on the account into which your dividends are paid. Once the dividends are paid into that account, they are automatically used to buy back stock. It becomes one less worry. The disadvantage, however, is that you lose control over the investment decisions.

Just keep in mind that a lot of countries don't allow dividend reinvestments, while the US does. So, if you're investing in a country like Australia or Brazil, they might not have this option. In this case, you should use the lump sum dividend reinvestment method.

Lump-Sum Manual Dividend Reinvestment

The second reinvestment option is where your dividends accumulate in cash. The dividends that you accumulate are added to your monthly savings, and that money is invested in dividend stocks that you choose.

As is the case with automatic dividend reinvestment, with manual reinvestment, you receive your dividend and direct it back to your investment so that it grows. However, in this case, the reinvestment is a large amount paid at once. Let's say your dividends accumulate into $10,000 cash. In lump-sum manual dividend reinvestment, you don't reinvest the money in dividend stocks as small amounts over time. Rather, you invest the whole $10,000 at once.

Be Patient and Give Your Snowball Strategy Time to Play Out

If you are the type of investor who wants to get rich quickly, you may find it very difficult to create a dividend snowball. It takes time for dividend compounding to play out. When creating a snowball, think long-term. See into the future, set out a solid plan, and forget about it. Being calm and patient is the best way to go about it.

Keep At It Until You Reach Your Dividend Crossover Point

Your dividend crossover point is that point where you reach the monthly or annual dividend income that you were targeting. You set up the crossover point as part of your snowball strategy. You should constantly check your position in relation to the crossover point that you set for yourself. You should do whatever it takes to make sure you achieve it. Achieving your crossover point usually shows that your portfolio is doing very well.

I hope this chapter has been an eye-opener to you. Many investors are taking advantage of dividend investing and making good money in the long term. If you are not the type of investor that wants instant results, you can try out dividend investing. As has been mentioned, patience is one of the most important virtues a dividend investor should possess. Dividend investing is also a good way to save up for your retirement, so if you are a future-oriented investor, you should start now.

Chapter Quiz/Summary

1. Dividend growth stocks have growing stock prices with same dividends. (True/False)
2. Dividend growth stocks have same stock prices with growing dividends (True/False)
3. Dividend growth stocks have growing stock prices with growing dividends (True/False)
4. Where do I check dividend history of a stock?
5. A company has a debt to asset ratio of 1.2. Is that good?
6. A company has a cash ratio of 0.4. Can I invest in this?
7. The dividend snowball strategy works if you keep selling your stocks (True/False).
8. The Automatic Dividend Reinvestment strategy means your dividends are automatically reinvested back into the stock (True/False).
9. Patience is the key to Dividend Investing (True/False).

Answers:

1. False
2. False
3. True
4. Dividendhistory.org
5. No. You should invest in stocks with debt to asset ratios below 0.5; preferably below 0.3
6. No. You should invest in stocks with cash ratios above 0.5; preferably above 1
7. False, the strategy relies on holding your stocks and reinvesting your dividends back into the stock.
8. True
9. True

Dividend Safety Stocks During a Market Crash

Stock market crashes are a difficult time to endure. Investors can cushion themselves from the hard effects of a crash by owning stocks of high quality and keeping a strong reserve of cash. Even during the economic downturn, these good companies will still be doing well, and they will still give their investors some sort of return.

Market crashes are nothing new. They have always been there. Many companies have survived them while still paying dividends to their investors. The dividends may not be high, but the fact that it is still there is very important.

The value of most portfolios takes a dip during market crashes; it is very painful to watch your investment portfolio value crater. If you are able to receive regular income during such a time, it makes a world of difference. Dividend stocks, therefore, come into the picture to save the day. This is one type of stock that you would find worthwhile to own during a market crash.

There are two very important principles that make dividends and market crashes a great combination.

- **Principle 1:** Dividends depend on the profitability of the business itself. They have nothing to do with the share price. This contributes greatly to the stability of dividends. Of course, there is no guarantee for dividends, but quality companies hardly ever cancel dividends because it affects the overall picture.

- **Principle 2:** The price of the shares in the stock market are simply a reflection of what people are willing to pay for the company's shares. It is a representation of human psychology and the forces of supply and demand—when people are irrationally selling, it can throw up anomalies. Share prices are volatile and variable. When you invest in dividends, you hope to have your shares for the rest of your life. It is the hope of every investor that the stocks they invest in will grow over time and will continue to pay them dividends. When a stock is doing well, there will be an increase in the share price. So, while you are making money through dividends, you can also decide to sell the share, which you will do at a profit.

The Investment Psychology of a Market Crash

Many investors find market crashes to be utterly scary because they can bring about swings to the paper wealth of an investor. The swings can be very dramatic, and it can lead to changes in how investors see the prospects of most companies. When a crash is ongoing, this is the perfect time to learn how top investors have survived them and master the art. An investor must learn to manage their psychology in order to learn how to survive a market crash.

Here are some of the psychological aspects of a market crash that will help an investor to do well in a market crash.

Focus on the Long Term

A successful investor, Warren Buffet views the market as if it is an individual. He calls it Mr. Market. On a daily basis, Mr. Market has prices at which he is willing to buy and sell shares and, if the investor is happy with such prices, they can do business. If they are not happy, they can ignore it.

A proverb by Warren Buffett, is one to keep in mind. "Buy when others are fearful; and sell when others are greedy". This is the right psychology to keep in mind. Just realize that your portfolio will go down; but if you invested in the right stocks, you would win in the long term. You will also receive a strong dividend income at this time.

If an investor is able to invest in high quality stocks, they are less affected by the changes that the market brings on a daily basis. Even if the market were to mark some of the stocks up or down, they would be affected very little by this; high quality stocks maintain their value. Some investors have come to view the market as a voting machine in the short run and as a weighing machine in the long run. The prices shift occasionally in the market, especially in the short term. These shifts sometimes present an incredible buying opportunity for investors. Top investors often ignore the noise of a market crash because their focus is usually on the long term.

Preparing For a Market Crash

Market crashes are nothing new to top investors. They've survived them before, and they have the assurance that they will survive them many more times. The timing however sometimes catches them off guard. Markets behave in a cyclical manner and, therefore, they are bound to move up and down with time. When a market is moving in such a rapid manner, this is a great opportunity to buy. Such opportunities can, however, be very short-lived and are only enjoyed by those investors who watch the market.

Top investors have created what they call shopping lists. These lists contain companies that they regard as great investments—when the price is right. With a strategy structured in this way, when there is a market crash, the investor can keep calm and act.

The most important thing is to keep cash in your brokerage account ready to be deployed in a market crash. This should be between 20% - 40% of your portfolio, depending on the market risk.

If the market has had a long period of upward movement, it's time to increase your cash holdings to close to 40%.

If the market has just had a mega crash, then start deploying your cash to buy stocks, and reduce it closer to a 20% holding.

Learning From a Market Crash

No one can really be totally prepared for a market crash. Even with all the preparation one may have done, crashes can still be difficult. A crash has the potential to destroy a lot of value, even if the investor chooses a portfolio of strong companies. While you may remain afloat, it may not be the same as if you are investing without a crash. In 1989, the Japanese Nikkei hit an all-time high. After a market crash hit, it has never again reached such highs.

A market crash can be a great learning opportunity. While it may be costly, the lessons can help you in the future. After going through a market crash, you should take stock of the things that you have learned and apply them to your investments. This makes you a stronger investor and you know better how to prepare for the next crash.

Utility stocks, healthcare stocks and consumer staples are known as defensive stocks. They are great during a market crash. A lot of them pay a decent dividend. A lot of them hold their value during a market crash. If they go down in value, they do a lot better than the rest of the market.

Utility Stocks

Utilities are a very important part of every society because life without access to these utilities seems unfathomable. Utility companies have taken advantage of the fact that they are overwhelmingly important. Utility companies are rated among some of the largest in the world. These large companies can generate stable and consistent revenues. This is why many investors are interested in investing in utility companies during a market crash.

What Are Utility Stocks?

These are the stocks of companies that provide basic utility services like water, electricity, waste management, gas, internet and telecommunication services. These are well established companies that consumers need for everyday survival. Some provide these services in a mixed bag. Investors prefer to have their money in these companies because utilities provide a consistent return.

Advantages of Utility Stocks

Whenever you are investing, you should make sure that you assess the advantages and disadvantages of stocks. Every type of investment carries some sort of risk and there is no investment that is risk-proof. When it comes to utility stocks, here are some of the most important advantages and disadvantages to consider.

Strong Dividend Payments

The cash flows of utility companies are usually predictable. For this reason, they pay generous dividend payments. It is quite common for investors to find utility stocks that have dividends above 5% with dividend payout ratios below 50%. Because of their strong dividends, utility stocks are great income plays. Whenever the company earns money, the investors, in turn, receive a paycheck. Always remember that every stock behaves differently, and you should try by all means to ensure that you research the utility company's history before you make an investment.

They Are Monopolies that Grow with the Population

Of course, experts do not agree with the idea that some people have those stocks can only go one way: up. A stock may be very strong, but the possibility of a decline cannot be completely ruled out. The utility sector, however, is more defined and investors are better able to see ahead. The future is quite clear. Utility companies fulfill the most basic needs of consumers. They have a strong customer base. This has helped utility companies to build a strong infrastructure—and they have the capacity to continue increasing it. Because the human population grows every day, these companies also continue to grow.

Utility companies in the United States have their target audience increasing by more than half a percent per year, which is also the population growth rate per year. This continuous expansion directly translates to a continuous increase in revenue. The companies continue to grow, which gives rise to operational efficiencies, which in turn reduce costs and go toward increasing profits.

Utility Stocks Act as Economic Shields

There are some places where economic recessions happen every 5-6 years and last for about a year on average. Whenever consumers develop concerns about an economic recession, they tend to cut down on their spending and save more money. The result on the corporate side is a reduction in revenue, and the stock values take a dive across the market. Utilities may have some slight dips here and there, but they are quite resilient during recessions.

When there are concerns about economic conditions, many consumers are usually grounded and stay at home. This leads to an increase in the use of utilities. Utility stocks take only slight dips because of continued usage; they recover quickly from these dips.

Disadvantages of Utility Stocks

Utility stocks are worth being considered by investors because of their impressive upsides. However, this does not imply that they do not have a downside. There are certain disadvantages that come with investing in the utility sector.

Relatively Slow Growth

Large utility companies are known for stable growth that favors long-term gains for investors, but the actual growth rate is very slow. The best utility stocks usually come from the largest and most well-established companies in the market. These companies depend on the growth in population for their growth in revenue. Therefore, their growth rates are very slow. They cannot be compared to something like the development of a new technology where revenues may increase dramatically. Therefore, if you are that investor who finds slow growth undesirable, you should look elsewhere other than the utility sector.

Potential for Losses

Utility stocks are commonly touted as stable investments. They are known to provide long-term growth and very stable dividends. However, investments can never be completely safe. It is possible to have losses from investing in the utility sector. The only way to be sure your money is completely safe is to keep it in cash. If you put it elsewhere, always leave room for the possibility of something befalling it.

There are some companies that fraudulently pose as if they are making profits when, in actual fact, they are not. Investors, on the other hand, can jump into investments with the belief that the possibility of returns is definite. You cannot be completely safe from losses, even when investing in the utility sector. This is why

I always emphasize the need to do thorough research before shelling out your money; and always keeping a reserve in hand.

How Much to Invest in Utility Stocks?

Allocation of money to different stocks that form your portfolio is an intimate process that depends on different aspects of your personal financial life. Your appetite for risk, your goals, and your investing style have a large bearing on the allocation of money. When your portfolio is well-diversified, it usually consists of both stocks, bonds and gold.

The 5% rule is very helpful to investors who want to create the best mix in their portfolios: do not put more than 5% of your investment into a single stock. If you are interested in utility stocks, not more than 5% of the total value of the portfolio should be in a single stock. You also do not have to max out the 5% on all of the utility stocks in your portfolio.

Diversify your income across multiple sectors. This is described more in detail in the chapter on "Setting up a Diversified Portfolio".

Your goals as an investor also have a great bearing. Your investment goals will differ from those of the next investor. For example, you might be interested in long-term retirement income, while the next investor is more into capitalizing on short-term momentum. Your investment goals will have a large bearing on the investment decisions that you make regarding the allocation of money among different assets in your portfolio.

Healthcare Defensive Stocks

Think about the last time you went to a doctor. Maybe that was yesterday. Maybe that was years ago. You paid the doctor, you paid for the medicines and maybe more. Would you not go if there was a recession?

If you really needed to go and you had the money, you would find a way to pay.

That's what makes healthcare stocks a great defensive play during a market crash.

Make sure you avoid healthcare innovation stocks that behave more like technology stocks and invest more in established healthcare companies. Pharmacy retail, biotech stocks and drug distribution stocks are examples of such stocks.

Consumer Staples

Consumer staples are stocks of companies that produce, distribute, and sell household goods, foods, beverages, grocery items etc. These are items that people are unable to eliminate from their budgets.

These are stocks like Coca-Cola, Kroger, Woolworths etc.

Since they have a regular income, they are able to provide a strong dividend that isn't cut during recessions.

How to Spot Safe Stocks with Low Debt?

It goes without saying that it is vital for an investor to filter out bad stocks from the defensive sector. Just because a company is in utilities, healthcare or consumer staples, doesn't mean that it is a good investment. Some companies have mismanaged their finances during the good times and are burdened with too much debt to be able to deal with a recession.

Safety stocks are those stocks that cushion you against unnecessary losses. They have lasting value. There are some stocks that are trendy—their value is based on hype. You should align yourself to stocks that have real, significant, and durable value. Some stocks are safe, even if their price is well below their actual value. For different reasons, stocks of great companies may go down. This is the best time to buy—bargains are also good in the stock market. For solid companies, the low value is usually a temporary slip.

How Do You Spot a Safe Stock?

Spotting a safe stock is dependent on several factors. Included in this section are some of the metrics to look at when identifying a safe stock.

Cash

A company should have cash at hand. The stocks of such a company are good because it is evident that the company has some money to spare. When sales dip, the cash held by the company keeps it going and it acts as a sort of insurance. Besides paying for the day to day running of the business, cash helps to pay for the growth of the company and also to maintain its dividends.

A good way to measure a company's cash on hand is the cash ratio. The cash ratio is the cash divided by the liabilities of the company. A good cash ratio is above 0.5. Ideally, you want a cash ratio to be above 1.

Little or No Debt

When a company has debt to pay off, it takes away the money that could otherwise have been used for profitable activities. Debt payments during bad times have the potential to drag a company under. A company should be able to channel all the resources that it makes to its growth. Repayment of debt reduces a company's potential for growth.

The Debt-to-Asset Ratio

The debt-to-asset ratio of a company is useful in the evaluation of a company's financial leverage. It is calculated by dividing the total liabilities of a company by the total assets. This ratio gives us a measure of how much a company is financed by debt and by funds that it wholly owns. If the debt is bigger, it means the company is not stable.

Debt/Equity = Total Liabilities/Total Assets

For example, if a company has $100,000 worth of liabilities, and $20000 assets, is highly leveraged and a very risky investment. If, on the other hand, a company has total liabilities of $50,000 and total assets of $100,000, it is a low-risk company and a very good investment.

Free Cash Flows

When a company has taken care of all its operating costs, the money that is left is the free cash flow. Free cash flow can be used to add to a company's cash and reduce its debt. The stocks of a company that does not spend more than it makes are safe. Companies that overspend may be successful in the short run, but in the long run, they will flame out.

Free cash flow is a subset of cash flow. It refers to the amount of cash that is left over when the company has paid all its expenses as well as capital expenditure. Free cash flow is easily calculated from the cash flow statement and is calculated as follows:

Free Cash Flow (FCF) = Operating Cash Flow (OCF) – Capital Expenditures

Example of Good Free Cash Flow

The following information is for XYZ Company for the fiscal year ending 2019.

Cash flow for Operating Activities = $1.608 billion

Capital Expenditures = $1.157 billion

The free cash flow of the company would therefore be calculated as follows:

FCF = $1.608 billion – $1.157 billion

= $450 million

As is evident, XYZ has a high free cash flow. This is good because it can be used to expand operations, deleverage the balance sheet, and pay dividends. If the free cash flow is able to cover these things, it is a good free cash flow. If, however, it is low enough to not cover some or all of these things, it means the free cash flow is not good enough.

Debt to Free Cash Flow

The best way to measure the strength of a company's cash flow is the debt to free cash flow ratio. The debt to free cash flow is a good way to check if the company has too much debt. If the debt to free cash flow is over 5, it is too highly leveraged.

In the above example, company XYZ has a debt of $900 million.

The debt to free cash flow is 2, which means that company XYZ has a good cash flow position. A debt to free cash flow ratio of 5 or below is considered a sign of financial strength.

Chapter Quiz/Summary

1. The market always goes up (True/False).
2. You should buy stocks only when everyone else is greedy and buying stocks (True/False).
3. A good way to prepare for a market crash is to hold 20-40% of your portfolio in cash (True/False).
4. Utility, healthcare defensive and consumer staples are good safety stocks during a market crash. (True/False).
5. Utility stocks always go up during a market crash. (True/False).
6. All utility and defensive stocks are safe during a recession. (True/False).
7. Two utility stocks have a debt to asset ratio of 0.2 and 0.7. Which one has a better debt position?
8. Two healthcare stocks have a debt to cash flow ratio of 3 and 6. Which one has a better cash flow position?

Answers:

1. False
2. False
3. True
4. True
5. False.
6. The one with a debt to asset ratio of 0.2
7. The one with a debt to cash flow ratio of 3

Dividend Capture Approach

Dividend capture is an investment strategy that focuses on the buying and selling of stocks that pay dividends within a particular time period. It is a short-term strategy.

The investor buys the stock just before its ex-dividend date in order to capture the dividend. The investor then sells the stock on or after the record date, at a higher price than the purchase price. The approach focuses on the receiving of the dividend and not just the selling of the stock at a profit.

For the dividend capture strategy to be worthwhile, the stock must be the one that pays a sizable dividend. The stocks should also have a very high trading volume to take advantage of the regular cash infusions that result from the payment of dividends. The strategy is often tackled with a one-size-fits-all approach. As explained, investors prefer to buy the stock just before the ex-dividend date and sell it on or after the date. This means that they do not hold the stock for a long time. Other investors sometimes decide to hold on to their stocks for a couple of days before they sell them off.

For the strategy to work, the stock must be sold at a price that is higher than the purchase price, not less. The strategy also works if the price of the stock drops below the amount of the dividend. That capital is no longer a part of the value of the company because it is allocated to shareholders. The strategy, however, does not always play out because it is not always the case that prices will drop below the price of the dividend. The share price of a company is dependent on several factors, and the dividend is just one of those things. Sometimes the share price can be affected by demand. The strategy is built on the premise that you do not need to hold the stock long-term for you to collect the dividend payment.

The traditional investment approach focused much on the buying of stocks and holding on to them until such a time when they appreciate. The dividend capture strategy is very popular with short term traders who have no intention to hold a stock for a long time but still want to capitalize on the price movements and payment of dividends. Sometimes the investor will hold the underlying stock for just a single day before they let it go, as long as the holding period is long enough to capture the dividend. This strategy is a very active strategy, which means the investor has to be actively engaged in the market to take note of the trends.

Most companies pay their dividends on a quarterly basis, but an investor who knows how to use the dividend capture strategy can get a dividend at least six times within the year. When the investor using the dividend capture strategy buys a dividend-paying stock, they have to sell it off thereafter and use the proceeds to buy another stock that is about to pay out a dividend. This sounds like it is easy, but it is not; there are several factors that contribute to making the strategy workable.

Many factors affect the effectiveness of the dividend capture strategy. For example, there are tax laws that stipulate that a stock must be held for 1 year before it gets a special tax rate. If it is not held for that period, it is taxed at the regular income tax rate for stockholders. In some cases, there can be very high trading costs which, at the end of the day, affect your profit margin. This can defeat the major goals of the dividend capture strategy. It is also the case that the stock price of the company that is preparing to make dividend payments usually goes up. The prices will decline soon after dividends are paid.

Despite the factors stated above, strategists almost always come up with ways to ensure that they make a profit out of the work that they do. The key to making it work is the timing because, if you get it right, you will make meaningful gains. The dividend capture strategy is mostly dependent on the history and the patterns of stocks. This will help you to determine what will possibly happen before and after the ex-dividend date. When you analyze these events in history, you may come up with the correct day to buy and sell the stock. While this strategy is used by a lot of experts to make money, if you are to venture into it for the first time, you need to be properly prepared, so you do not wind up with staggering losses.

Special considerations to make include the fact that when the stocks are heavily trading, the price is less likely to reduce before the ex-dividend date. Also, if a stock is on a strong uptrend, it is likely to appreciate. This will result in the investor getting a dividend as well as the profit of the sale. On the other hand, stock prices can fall far below what you expect after the ex-dividend date. This may prompt the investor to sell the stock at a time that is more profitable, not on the ex-dividend date. They may decide to wait until the stock has gained value. This may be a few days after the ex-dividend date, but in some cases, the price may continue to fall.

Real-World Examples of the Dividend Capture Approach

Here are some examples of real-world uses of the dividend capture approach.

Apple

Let's say that if Apple, in June of 2027, went ex-dividend after they declared a dividend of $0.51. On the day before the ex-dividend date, the stock closed at $147.23. It was possible to purchase shares at this price or less. If the investor were to hold the shares at the ex-dividend date, they would be entitled to the dividend of $0.51. On the day following the ex-dividend date, the stock opened at $148.06. This means that if the trader sold the shares, they would lock in a profit of $0.83 on top of the $0.51 dividend they would have received per share. At the time this scenario happened, Apple was in a strong uptrend. So, the trader made a profit of $1.31 per share from the trade.

United Airlines

Let's say United Airlines declared a $0.5025 dividend on the same day that it went ex-dividend. On the same day, the stock closed at $69.72. On the following day, the stock price was at $69.49. This means that the trader would sell the stock at a loss of $0.23, but still receive a dividend of $0.5025. At the time, the stock was in a trendless period. So, the trader made a net profit of $0.2525 per share from the trade.

Advantages and Disadvantages of the Dividend Capture Strategy

On the surface, a dividend capture strategy may seem to be straightforward and simple, but the case is not always so. There are several advantages and disadvantages to the strategy that you might want to learn about if you are interested in the strategy.

Advantages

Here are some of the advantages of the dividend capture strategy:

- The strategy allows the investor to make quick entry and exit. This means that your trades are handled in a matter of days, and you are done. This eliminates the risks of having your stocks decline in value while you still hold them. Usually, when that happens, it will become very difficult to sell the stock because the value will have gone down.

- The dividend capture strategy be used successfully in any market condition, as long as the investor times the trades correctly.

- There are several ways to implement this strategy and an investor can choose which one works better for them. The investor is free to decide when to sell the stock, that is, on or after the ex-dividend date, depending on what the trade-offs look like. This means that most of the decisions concerning a particular trade lie in the hands of the investor.

- One other advantage of the dividend capture strategy is that it is definite that you will find dividend-paying stocks in the market on any given day. If you are a fan of this strategy, you can be sure of continuity because there are stocks being sold every other day. This is the reason why most day traders make use of this strategy. The dividend-paying stocks are available to them every single day.

Disadvantages

The disadvantages of the dividend capture strategy include the following:

- When you employ the dividend capture strategy, you have a higher chance of making a profit. But the money that you make can be beyond certain thresholds and can be taxable at a higher rate. The taxes can really be a burden and weigh down on your earnings.

- All dividend stocks have the tendency of plummeting on the ex-dividend date. Unless the investor sets up a strategy that helps them to counter the decline in prices, they will be forced to wait for the recovery of the stock prices before they sell the stocks.

- While the strategy may be well-timed and profit the trader, the transaction costs can be very high as to negatively impact the profitability of the strategy. If the costs are high, the investor may unknowingly incur losses because the costs will eat into the profits the investor has made.

- The prices of stocks can be very inconsistent because of volatility in the market. This hampers the effectiveness of the strategy because the investor may predict the capital gains to be at a certain level during the dividend capture strategy. However, if the market is very volatile, the capital gains may deviate from what is expected and this will affect the capital gains of the investor. Sometimes it may lead to losses.

Other Criticisms of the Dividend Capture Strategy

The dividend capture strategy has been criticized in some cases for not producing tax advantages. The dividend returns are taxed at the ordinary capital gains tax rate of the investor. The reason is that dividend capture trades are not held long enough to benefit from the tax advantages and favorable treatment that the long-term investor receives from their dividends. This can however be tackled if the investor is wise enough to employ the strategy using a tax-advantaged account such as an individual retirement account.

It is also very difficult to account for the transaction costs of this strategy. While it is very dangerous to trade without accounting for these costs, it is also very difficult to account for them. Companies are paying dividends on a daily basis and this strategy is a very active one; the trader could have to account for trading costs on a daily basis. You will also find that the more active the strategy, the more commissions are paid.

The dividend capture strategy can be time-consuming, but it is very worthwhile. Depending on how much time you have to spare in your day, you can make time for day trading on a daily basis. All you need to do is to learn about the basics of this strategy such as how to time the buying and selling of stocks. When you master the art, you can start off with lower capital and increase as you sharpen your skills.

I hope that having gone through this chapter; you are now well-versed with the dividend capture strategy. It may be difficult for you to engage in it as a college student because it is capital intensive and very active. You must make a high initial outlay to be able to trade and you have to make time to actively engage in the market on a daily basis. This, however, should not scare you away. Because, not in all cases, you don't have to do it yourself. You can make use of the services of experts and professionals who will help you to carry out your trades and time the market. All you must do is to ensure that the costs do not overshadow the profits that you make. Make sure you understand the risks involved in this method.

Chapter Quiz/Summary

1. A dividend capture approach involves buying a stock after the dividend is paid. (True/False)
2. A dividend capture approach involves buying a stock before the ex-dividend date. (True/False)
3. A dividend capture approach involves selling a stock after the payment date. (True/False)
4. A dividend capture approach involves selling a stock after the record date. (True/False)
5. A stock C is at $0.61 on December 3rd. The ex-dividend date is December 5th. The record date is December 6th; and the payment date is December 20th. The stock is at $0.7 on December 6th and $0.65 on the payment date. The dividend paid is $0.06 per share.
   a. On what date do you buy for the Dividend capture approach?
   b. On what date do you sell?
   c. What's the profit from the dividend capture trade?
6. What is the risk to the dividend capture strategy?

Answers

1. False
2. True
3. False
4. False; it can be on the record date
5. A. December 3rd or 4th

   B. December 6th or after.

   C. ($0.7-$0.61) +$0.06=$0.15 profit per share (if selling on record date)
6. The stock can decrease in value after the ex-dividend date.

Dividend Investment Traps

There are many times when investors just select stocks and press the buy button without giving it a second thought. This is especially easy for them if they have made a number of successful trades in the past. However, it will not be long before Wall Street gives you a reality check, because stocks can and do crash in the short term.

Other investors have come to think that they are unlucky, and investing is not for them. They have seen their picks going lower and lower losing a lot of money. Sometimes they buy high and sell low, and when they do that, they incur losses. As if that is not enough, when they exit the market, the prices suddenly shoot up. This is because of investment mistakes that investors make without knowing. This chapter will go over these.

Dividend investing is quite sophisticated and such mistakes are quite expected. This is one strategy that pays well but is complex in its nature. When you fail to use the dividend investing strategy properly, it can brew disaster for the investor. If an investor learns some of the pitfalls that affect investors, they can avoid them. It goes a long way in safeguarding the investor's money. Here are some of the common dividend investing mistakes that are made.

Mistake 1: The High Dividend Trap

While coming across dividend stocks, you might come across stocks that have an extremely high dividend yields. Sometimes, you might see a dividend yield of 15% or 20%. These yields sound impressive; and you might think you've just struck gold.

However, the issue is that the company might be using all their profits to pay dividends. Or even worse, it might be financing its dividends through debt.

How do you tell the difference? Is it a really strong company that has more money than it needs? Or is it a failing business that's trying to trap investors by luring them with abnormally high dividends?

Let's have a look.

Dividend Yields Can Be Misleading If a Stock Just Crashed

As we learned earlier, the dividend yield is annual dividend percentage yield paid by the company.

The dividend yield can be a perilous trap if you are not careful. When calculating the dividend yield, the denominator is the price per share. If the price per share goes down, while the dividends remain unchanged, this means that the dividend yield should rise. For example, let's say Chevron paid of dividend of $3 when it's share price was $100. That's a dividend yield of 3%. However, the month after the dividend was paid, the share price crashes to $50. The dividend yield now becomes ($3/50)*100 = 6%. The dividend yield now shows as 6%.

Date	Dividend Paid	Chevron price	Trailing Dividend Yield
March 6 (Payment Date)	$3	$100	3/100*100 = 3%
April 6 (Current Date)		$50	3/50*100 = 6%
June 6 (Next Payment Date)	??	??	??

This may or may not be a buying opportunity. If the share price crashed because Chevron was losing business, maybe next time they can't afford to pay $3 dividend. You won't get a 6% dividend. So, the 6% dividend is a mirage.

If the share price crash was due to some other external factors and Chevron's earnings are still great, then they might still be able to pay the dividend of $3. It's important to understand why the share price crashed. Using this information together with fundamental analysis helps you to better figure out how the stock may be behaving.

When you perform a proper analysis, you will be able to develop a holistic view of the performance of the company. You will also be clear about its liquidity and solvency. Liquidity is a measure of how quickly a company can convert its assets into cash. Solvency measures the ability of a company to meet its obligations. The payment of dividends is done out of cash and the cash is made from earnings. The company should, therefore, have a history of consistency when it comes to earnings and earnings growth. You should never fall into the trap of only observing high dividends while turning a blind eye to duration.

There are a lot of things to observe about a company besides the high dividends. A company can get into debt and, for the reason of wanting to save face, still pay dividends. You must find out if the company is in any form of large debt before you invest. This might be an indicator that the high dividend payouts may not last for long. It would be bad for you to invest in a company that purports high earnings, only to find the earnings falling significantly a few months into the investment.

The payout ratio is a financial metric that is used to present the proportion of the earnings that the company pays out to its shareholders in the form of dividends. The payout ratio is expressed as a percentage of the total earnings of the company.

In some cases, the payout ratio represents the dividends that the company pays out, expressed as a percentage of the cash flow of the company. The payout ratio can sometimes be referred to as the dividend payout ratio.

When a company has a low payout ratio, the implication is that the company is reinvesting most of its earnings into expanding its operations. If the payout ratio is above 100%, it shows that the company is paying out more in dividends than its earnings can sustain. This is often viewed by many as unsustainable and may be an indication that the company is using other means, such as using debt, to source the funds to pay dividends. The payout ratio is calculated as follows:

Payout ratio = Dividend Income / Net Income

The payout ratio is a good metric for determining whether the earnings of a company are growing or not. A lower payout ratio also implies that the company is earning enough to sustain the dividends it is paying out.

We ideally want a dividend payout ratio less than 50%; and avoid companies with payout ratio greater than 70%.

Example 1: Good Payout Ratio That is Growing

Consider the following information for company ABC:

Details	2016	2015
Dividend Payment	50,000	40,000
Net Income	325,0000	300,000
Dividend Payout Ratio	**15.38%**	**13.33%**

There are two important things to note here.

One is the payout ratio is only 13-15%. This is low. That means that the company has plenty of extra money to invest in growing its business.

The payout ratio has also increased in the year 2016 as compared to the year 2015. If the company is still in the growth stages, this is a good sign. The payout ratio indicates that the payment of dividend is sustainable and can be consistent.

Example 2: Bad Payout Ratio

Consider the following information for XYZ Company:

Details	2016	2015
Dividend Payment	240,000	210,000
Net Income	325,0000	300,000
Dividend Payout Ratio	73,85%	70%

An analysis of the payout ratios above shows that the company is distributing more than half of the total earnings to the payment of dividends. This means the company has low retained earnings. The increase in the payout ratio in the year 2016 shows that the company has less retained earnings in comparison to the previous year. We want to avoid investing in this company as it may be a dividend trap.

Mistake 2: Buying Low-Quality Stocks

The desire to buy cheap stocks can culminate in big losses. For an inexperienced investor, it can be very tempting to go for stocks that are cheap because you might have low capital to start investing with. Stocks with a lower share price can include penny stocks, which may cost less than $5 per share. While these stocks may appear like they are the real deal, you are exposing yourself to a great deal of risk. Of course, the idea is that, when you invest in such companies, you are getting enough exposure to the equities world without having to invest a fortune. However, the truth of the matter is that, even if you do not have much capital, you do not have to specifically focus on low-cost investments.

There are some problems that you can encounter from trading in stocks of low price and quality. Penny stocks take up most of the space in the low-quality and low-price stock world. Penny stocks are usually unregulated and there is not much information provided about them to the investor. The trading volumes for stocks that are cheap are usually very low. It is very difficult to buy and sell such stocks and you may find yourself stuck with certain stocks and failing to get them off your hands for a profit. They are also very vulnerable to scams.

If you are to be a good investor, you must always remember that a low price does not always translate to good value. Some stocks may surely have a low share price but, at the end of the day, you will realize that the stock may not even be worth that low price. Stocks can be priced low to ensnare unsuspecting investors, but you will later find out that the company may have serious problems that it is struggling to get out of. In some cases, the company will show very little potential for growth. Remember, in the equities market, karma has it that you usually get what you pay for. If you buy cheap stocks, you can be sure to get low quality.

Mistake 3: Holding onto Stocks Past Their Due Date

It is true that some stocks can be held forever. Think about Coca-Cola or Walmart. These companies have growing businesses that are very competitive and do well in all types of markets. However, this is very rare. And, even for those companies, we need to monitor their earnings to ensure that they have earnings growth and net income growth.

The timing of how long a time is healthy for you to hold onto a stock is usually out of your control. There are many companies that have offered stock options to their employees but, by the time the companies folded, they had decreased in value. There are many factors that may cause the stocks that an investor holds to decrease in value. It could be a new competitor that enters the market or, maybe, a new innovation and development that makes your company's' products obsolete. Sometimes you may try hard to keep your investment afloat, but the value of the company will continue to fall, and you end up losing.

Many investors have a terrible time letting go of certain stocks. The reason why people tend to hold on to a stock is that they are afraid of missing out. The stock market can be a gamble at times. The investor may be thinking that if they hold on a little longer, they might get more income. You should know that holding on to a stock for too long does not maximize its value but rather exposes you to more risk in the market.

Other Dividend Investing Mistakes to Avoid

Besides the mistakes explained above, there are other dividend investing mistakes that are often made by investors. The effects of these mistakes may just be as far-reaching as other mistakes and may cause the investor to lose out on their investment. Here are some such mistakes:

Misusing an Investment Strategy

There are a number of dividend investing strategies out there, and each investor is attracted to a strategy of their own. Strategies are chosen by investors who believe that they are the best for them. But this may, however, not be the case in your situation. This is one misstep that is very dangerous, and you should avoid it. You must make a comprehensive assessment of your situation and other important financial metrics. This will help you to come up with the best strategy for you. Appreciate the fact that not every strategy works for everyone. Learn as much as you can about dividend investing so that you are better able to figure out what works for you and what doesn't.

For example, a long-term dividend investor might want to avoid using the dividend capture strategy; while a trader might want to only use the options strategy and dividend capture strategy.

Misjudging Your Financial Needs

This is a common mistake among new investors. They are often fooled into thinking that dividend investing is rewarding enough to replace their paycheck. You need to run your numbers well and be conservative in your figures. You should never invest in dividends with the expectation that the dividends will cover all your living expenses. You have to include a factor of safety in your calculations. For example, if you living expenses are $4000 a month; you want to get a dividend income of $6000 a month (a factor of safety of 50%) before feeling comfortable in retirement.

Investors often underestimate their expenses and, at the same time, overestimate their dividend income. This is another pitfall. You should always be careful with the estimation of your expenses and your future needs. You should allow enough of a margin to allow for a comfortable lifestyle.

Failing to Reinvest Dividends

Dividend investments often grow if the investor masters the ability to reinvest dividends, even when they have demanding needs like funding their lifestyle. Reinvesting dividends can be vital. It causes you to create a dividend snowball. For any dividend investing strategy to work, you need to reinvest as much as possible and not take out of it before it has grown. Rather, wait until you can really afford to spend the money before you do so.

If you must live off your dividends, try to make sure that your needs are not in excess of the dividends you are receiving. If you manage to cover your needs and have some excess funds, you can reinvest them. As your dividends grow, you will discover that there will be more to reinvest. One good thing to do is to minimize your monthly budget. Make sure your needs are as lean as possible and let go of anything that is not necessary. Align yourself to developing your finances for the future.

Investing in Companies That Are Not Growing

Before making an investment, most investors often look at the stock price. The stock price by itself is an irrelevant metric in determining the perfect trade for you. It will not help you in any way in determining the perfect investment strategy. The best thing to focus on is the dividend yield. Instead of looking at the chart of prices, it is better to look at the historical dividend payments of the company. You should not focus on identifying companies with stock prices that are rising, but on those whose dividend payments are regular and consistent. If you are dealing with growth strategies, looking at stock prices would be ideal, but with dividend investing, much of the focus should be on consistent dividend payments. With dividend investing, regular dividend payments are a better sign of growth than stock prices.

I hope that this chapter has helped to enlighten you on some dividend investing mistakes that are made by most investors. It is not good for you to venture into investing without knowledge. This will cause you to encounter significant pitfalls. As a young investor, you are making investments with vital capital, so you need to avoid any mistakes that will reduce your chances of losing money.

Chapter Quiz/Summary

Dividend Yield = (Dividend Paid / Current Stock Price) * 100

1. What happens to the dividend yield when a company doubles its dividends?
2. What happens to the dividend yield when a company stock crashes 50% in one day?
3. A stock X paid $1 per share dividend in September when the stock price was $100. It rose to $200 per share in October. What is the new dividend yield?
4. What is the one key to accumulating a dividend snowball?
5. How do I keep track of a company's performance?
6. What is the factor of safety that I need to keep in mind while coming up with a dividend income threshold?
7. If my living expenses are $3000 a month, how much dividend income do I need to retire?

Answers:

1. Dividend yield doubles
2. Dividend yield doubles
3. 0.5%
4. Reinvesting dividends in quality companies with growing dividends
5. Monitor earnings every quarter
6. 50% factor of safety
7. $4500 per month (50% factor of safety)

Setting up a Diversified Dividend Portfolio

When it comes to setting up a long-term portfolio, diversification is crucial. You should never make forget about diversification. It is vital to ensure that you are not overexposed in the market because you will not get all your investment decisions right. Some of them will go wrong; diversification will cushion you. This chapter will take you deeper into the concept of diversification and will help you with the process.

What is Portfolio Diversification?

Portfolio diversification is an age-old principle of investment that states that an investor should never put all their eggs in one basket. The concept is that the investor should broaden their horizon by not investing in a small number of stocks in the same sector. Instead, one can invest in a variety of dividend stocks in different industries, in utility, mining, technology etc. We will specifically discuss asset allocation, but it is very important to understand that the major aim here is to spread risk across asset classes, markets, and economies to safeguard your investment.

The Importance of Diversification

Diversification, as already mentioned, goes a long way in avoiding exposure to a small number of assets. When you invest in a small or single type of asset your exposure to risk is great; if anything happens that brings down the value of the portfolio, your whole investment will be affected. When you invest across different asset classes, tap into different markets, and even go across countries, you spread your risks greatly. If one part of your portfolio does not do well, the others will, and you will be cushioned from risk.

The risk of short-term market volatility can affect your portfolio greatly. When you diversify your portfolio, you greatly reduce risks that have to do with short-term volatility. Some asset classes may be affected, but because you have a wide array of them in your portfolio, the others will cushion you against total loss. In some cases, you can make capital investment plans that sometimes do not go according to plan. Diversification protects you from the negative effects.

It is apparent that markets will always alternate between bull and bear markets. Bull markets are good for investors because there is not much negativity in the movement of prices; as long as the investment is set up well, the investor is almost guaranteed to get good returns. In bear markets, however, you will find that your portfolio will be declining gradually in value. If the bear market is prolonged, you may end up with losses. Diversification will help you to reduce the effects of a prolonged bear market because the assets that you hold will not be affected the same.

Sometimes the selection of stocks for investment is more like a gamble. You may select a stock that will not do well. In a diversified portfolio, you will find a good stock selection and some that are not so good. The good ones will cover your investment from the effects of bad stock selections. With diversification, you also get to enjoy the benefits of income generation and capital gains. The investor is also able to build their portfolio and align it in relation to long-term financial goals and their level of risk tolerance.

Diversify Across Different Industries

There are sectors that seem to be the real deal, but investors that are risk-averse will choose to diversify across different industries and sectors. Some prefer to niche down within a particular industry. For example, in the energy industry one can specifically choose to invest in gas, oil, and other forms of energy. If one form of energy does not do well and prices are tumbling, there obviously will be another form that is doing well.

Diversifying across different sectors is very important especially if you are dealing with the stock market. Certain sectors will perform better or worse than others. During the heated days of the coronavirus pandemic in 2020, many industries and sectors were affected, but they did not all take the blow the same. While the airline industry and restaurant sector were hit badly during this time, other sectors, such as health care and technology, did extremely well during that time. The large manufacturing companies that engaged in the manufacture of health kits and protective material did very well. If one investor had stocks in such a company and another company in the transport sector that was not doing well, the total performance of the portfolio would still not be that bad.

Diversifying Across Different Asset Classes

A well-diversified portfolio incorporates various asset classes. Such a variety comes in handy in enhancing your exposure to assets that belong to different classes. However, the wider asset variety makes it difficult for investors to determine the asset allocation splits that might work best for them. While expanding across different asset classes is of paramount importance, be sure to take some time to acquaint yourself with the specific asset classes that are accessible to you. If you are a dividend investor, prior knowledge with regard to how other stocks that are part of your portfolio assist you to protect your dividend stocks. Find out the level of risk that is involved for all the asset classes in a bid to maintain a balanced portfolio.

Blue-chip stocks are perceived to have a low-risk level because these companies are established and are very stable. They are usually leaders and pacesetters in their sectors. Growth stocks have a higher level of risk because they are usually thought of as stocks that are behind unproven products. The companies may not have been around for long and may not have established a reasonable track record. In the fixed income sector, you can also consider bonds which are at the forefront of the sector. This asset class also comes with its own risks and rewards; you might want to look at them before you add them to your portfolio. There are also assets like US Treasuries. These areas are as risk-free as anyone would expect.

When you diversify across these different asset types, you will have better peace of mind because you hedge against risk. You do not have to worry about what will happen if the market goes in the opposite direction than what you expect. Some people also include commodities like gold and other precious metals. These help you to hedge against what is going on in the traditional stock market. Diversification will work very well if it is carefully structured. All you need to do is to understand the nuts and bolts of each financial instrument that you intend to include in your portfolio.

Our Ideal Asset Allocation for a Dividend Portfolio

The best way through which you can balance risk and reward is through asset allocation. With this strategy you will come up with the perfect mix of assets and financial instruments in your portfolio. The aim in all this is to build a portfolio that helps you to achieve the ultimate goal of growing your wealth over time. You should be able to strike an equilibrium between risk and profit potential. Of course, each investor has a different risk profile and financial objectives. To be more specific, the asset allocation may differ due to age and time horizon. This section will focus specifically on the ideal asset allocation for a college student.

People can go to college at any time, which is the reason why you will find people of different ages in college. However, most college students are young and have several decades before they must live off their retirement savings. These people usually employ asset allocation strategies that are more aligned to financial instruments that have a greater risk. This means that your focus may be a lot more on stocks, especially dividend-paying stocks, than low-risk financial instruments.

On the other hand, if you have worked for the better part of your life and are nearing retirement, you will want to allocate more of the portfolio to fixed-income assets that have a lower risk profile.

We have two portfolios that we recommend to generate dividend income, based on your age and risk profile.

Dividend Portfolio 1

If you have a portfolio that is based on an income model, it means that all, or most, of the assets have minimum risk. They generate regular income which comes in the form of dividend stocks and stock appreciation. Here is the portfolio allocation that I use for dividend investments:

- 30% Commodity Dividend Stocks

- 30% Utilities Dividend Stocks

- 40% Technology Dividend Stocks

This strategy gives you a diversified income of dividends across a variety of industries. For your Commodity portion, you want to be a little more active and invest during times when commodities are at the bottom of their commodity cycle. For example, you should buy commodity dividend stocks when oil is $20 per barrel and sell when it goes over $100. This requires being more of an active investor. We also need to invest in companies with solid balance sheets, like companies with strong dividends and low debt to asset ratio.

Utility stocks generally provide high dividends and have a Buy and Hold strategy. They may sink during recessions, but they hold up better than the general market, among the last stocks to crash and the first to recover.

The Technology section of the portfolio has the best growth potential. In this sector, we recommend looking at dividend growth stocks; that have growing dividend yields during recessions. These stocks must have strong cash flows, earnings and low debt. Avoid stocks that prefer doing cash buybacks instead of paying dividends.

Invest in stocks that have growing revenue, net profit and growing dividends.

Dividend Portfolio 2

This portfolio has less risk as compared to the previous one. It has a lower allocation to technology and higher allocation to utility stocks. There is also a 20% allocation to inflation indexed bonds or i-bonds.

- 10% Commodities Dividend Stocks

- 20% i- bonds

- 20% Technology Dividend Stocks

- 50% Utility Dividend Stocks

The 20% in i-Bonds bonds adds a little stability to the portfolio. It is indexed to inflation. So, if inflation is at 8%, it'll pay you 8%. If inflation is at 4%, it'll pay 4%. The only disadvantage is you can only invest a maximum of $10000 per person per year. You can increase your investments over time. i-bonds are only issued by the US Government and require a social security number. Also, note that there are penalties for withdrawals before 5 years.

Other alternatives to i-bonds are Treasury Inflation Protected Securities (TIPS).

Disadvantages of Portfolio Diversification

Diversifying portfolios is ideal for most investors, but it does have its drawbacks. One of the drawbacks is time. Having to diversify across different asset classes can be very time-consuming. You must take time to study the markets and assets to find out which ones fit your desires and can be part of your portfolio. Besides being time-consuming, it can be very costly if the broker charges flat commissions. As an investor with a day job, you wouldn't want to engage in diversification if it costs you a lot of money.

Maintaining Your Portfolio

The Importance of Rebalancing

When you are investing through an actively managed fund, you will have no trouble with having to constantly check the balancing of your portfolio. The balance that you strike at the beginning, however, is not the same as that which will prevail until the end. There are a lot of changes that happen in the market, and you may have to occasionally rebalance your portfolio so that you continue to get positive returns. Maintaining a big allocation of assets that are underperforming may weigh down your portfolio.

Now, let's look at an example. Let's say you choose to invest in Dividend Portfolio 1. Three months after you set the allocation, there is a huge increase in your commodity stocks, and a crash in the technology stocks. Your commodity portion becomes 50% of your portfolio, while your technology section becomes 20%. In this case, you should sell some of the stocks in your commodity portfolio; and reinvest those in technology dividend stocks or utility dividend stocks. This is especially the case if your commodities are at the top of their commodity cycle.

Now, let's look at a second example. Let's say you bought Apple stock. You followed our rule and made sure it wasn't more than 5% of your portfolio. 1 year later, Apple stock has tripled due to the release of its new iPhone. So, now it's 15% of your portfolio. It may be difficult, but it's time to sell some Apple stock to ensure it's still at 5% of your portfolio.

So how often do you rebalance? Do it every year. Sometimes, in times of high market volatility, you can do it every 6 months.

So, the two takeaways of rebalancing your portfolio are:

1. Ensure that no single is more than 5% of your portfolio.

2. Rebalance your portfolio every 6 months to a year to ensure that you maintain a balanced portfolio.

Earnings and Net Income

Once you've invested in individual stocks, it is important to review earnings of the companies you've invested in every quarter. That's why we recommend no more than 10 stocks in your entire portfolio.

Now, how do we do this? It's easy to do this in Google. Just type in the name of the company you want to check out earnings for.

Etsy	Etsy Inc >
	NASDAQ: ETSY

Quarterly financials

DEC 2021	SEPT 2021	JUNE 2021	M/ >

(USD)	Dec 2021	Y/Y
Revenue	717.14M	16.18% ↑
Net income	161.56M	6.76% ↑
Diluted EPS	1.11	2.78% ↑
Net profit margin	22.53%	6.36% ↓
Operating income	143.98M	10.81% ↓
Net change in cash	160.79M	62.21% ↑
Cash on hand	-	-
Cost of revenue	208.97M	38.59% ↑

Check out the parts highlighted in green above.

157

First, ensure that the earnings are **Year/Year (Y/Y)** and not Quarter/Quarter. **Y/Y** ensures that you remove any seasonal variation.

a. Revenue should be higher. This is the case for Etsy; which is a good sign.

b. Net income should be higher. Net income is higher, which is good. But notice that it is growing slower than the revenue, which is a warning sign.

c. Cost of revenue increase should be negative or lower than revenue increase. In this case, we see that cost of revenue is increasing at 39%; which is more than double the revenue increase. This is a warning sign for investors and should be monitored. The company could struggle in an inflationary environment.

Monitor earnings to see how your stocks are performing over time. It is normal for companies to have lower income during a recession. But it's an alarming sign if revenues are going down while cost of revenues are going up.

We generally do not want to sell quality stocks that are paying us good dividends. But there are occasions when good companies go bad. Think of General Motors, General Electric, Lehmann Brothers etc. Most of the time we can avoid bad companies by checking out their debt profiles. But sometimes, they get bad over time or just get unlucky. So, earnings are a great way to spot that.

In conclusion, portfolio diversification is one of the concepts that are very important for an individual who wants to make the most out of their investing journey and reduce risk. This concept has been discussed extensively in this chapter to help start out. Diversification, however, does not guarantee that things will always go the way you plan. Things may not turn out so well for some asset classes, but diversification does improve your chances of achieving your financial objectives within your intended time horizon.

Chapter Quiz/Summary

1. You should invest your entire dividend portfolio in commodities because they pay high dividends. (True/False)
2. You should invest your entire portfolio in Apple stock, because it has been going up for the last 10 years. (True/False)
3. You should invest all your dividend portfolio in technology stocks because that is the future. (True/False)
4. You should maintain a diversified, rebalanced portfolio in Technology, Commodities and Utilities that pays you a strong dividend income. (True/False)
5. If one of the stocks in your portfolio goes up 100x, you should just hold it forever as it may keep going up. (True/False)
6. How often should you rebalance your portfolio?

Answers:

1. False
2. False
3. False
4. True
5. False, you should sell some to maintain a diversified portfolio
6. Every 6-12 months

Tax Strategies

Sometimes the return on investment is greatly reduced by investment expenses and brokerage fees. Taxes, however, are a bigger drag on investment returns. Investors who overlook tax issues tend to leave a lot of money on the table. Many investors will only look at taxes when they are nearing year's end. You should not let that happen to you. You must learn as much as you can about taxes and keep the information in mind throughout the whole year. Markets change frequently and it is wise to make tax-wise changes in your investment.

When you hold stocks and other assets that will remain in your hands for over a year, you should hold them in taxable accounts so that you enjoy the advantage of long-term capital gains. Dividend-paying stocks should also be held in taxable accounts. When you hold assets that earn short term capital gains and taxable interest, you should hold them in tax deferred accounts.

Many companies pay dividends when the dividend payments do not deter them from meeting their obligations when they become due. The dividends are also paid out if the company's assets are not less than its liabilities. When there are serious threats to the solvency of the company, that company will not pay dividends. Companies will always want to be proactive in the payment of dividends so that they can reduce the exposure of their assets.

Find Tax Free Dividends

The taxability of dividends depends on several factors. It depends on your residence and your level of income. In some countries, certain types of dividend investments are tax free to the investor. Given that there are 196 countries in the world and their laws keep changing, we cannot go through this in detail. It's best to consult a local accountant and ask them about tax free dividend sources in your area.

Changing your tax residency

As you may already know, different countries have different rules on taxing income. The same goes for taxing dividend income. As of 2022, there are several countries that do not tax dividend income. Hong Kong, Estonia and Latvia are a few countries that do not tax dividend income.

Also keep in mind that there are countries that do not have a capital gains tax rate; like Singapore, New Zealand, Switzerland etc.

Of course, there are many other reasons why one may want to move countries that have nothing to do with tax rate; but that's beyond the scope of this book.

It's just a good idea to ensure what your options are; and keep up to date on these options just in case you're looking to get more for your money.

Investing in a tax advantaged account (Roth IRA in the US)

Undisputedly, retirement accounts are the best way to save on taxes. These accounts are accessible to most people and experts also recommend them whenever the reduction of taxes is in question. When you invest in a retirement account, you reduce your taxable income and, at the same time, your investments will grow tax free until the time you retire.

List of Tax Advantaged Programs Across the Globe

USA – IRA, Roth IRA

Canada – Registered Retirement Savings Plan

Australia – Self Invested Super Fund

UK – Self-Invested Pension Plan

India – Personal Provident Fund (PPF)

Do Not Sell Assets

Not selling assets is a commonsense approach that helps you to avoid adding to your income when it is inconvenient for you to do so. One good formula for avoiding taxes on investments is not selling the assets that you hold until you are in a position that allows you to increase your income. The selling of your assets should be strategic. The most significant investments should be sold in years when you have the lowest income. This will have the effect of stabilizing your long-term income. You will be able to stay in the same tax bracket despite having earned a lot of money.

A Flexible Spending Account

If your employer offers one, you can try out a flexible spending account. This account allows you to funnel your paycheck directly into a tax-advantaged account. You can use the money in a flexible spending account to cover most out-of-pocket medical expenses. A variety of medical items are available to you through this account.

Deferring Bonus Checks

At the end of the year, a year-end bonus increases your income and puts you in a tax bracket that is much higher. In order to avoid this, you can defer your bonus check and ask your employer to pay you in the first month of the following year. The money will still get to you but, at the same time, you will have evaded an inflated income. It works better if your employer agrees to it and is not bothered. This really works best if you plan to quit your job the next year and your taxable income will be lower in the next year.

Other Tax Strategies

1. Don't sell within 1 year – Get Long Term Capital Gains

Investors are rewarded in most countries for holding stocks long term. In the United States, capital gains for stocks that are held for 1 year or longer are taxed at 15% instead of 25% (as of 2022). This is to disincentivize short term trading. So, try your best to keep your winning stocks for at least 1 year before selling.

2. Selling losing stocks during a profitable year

You can reduce your capital gains tax for a year with some capital losses. So, let's say you've made $3000 when you sold Microsoft stock earlier in the year. Come tax time, you notice that your Tesla stock is down $2000. If you sell your Tesla stock now, your capital gains reduce from $3000 to $1000 ($3000-$2000).

This is a great strategy to reduce your taxes during great bull markets.

3. Selling winners during a market crash year

If you've made some capital losses during a year, some countries (like the USA) allow you to write off that against your income (for up to $3000). So, if you made $50000 last year, and you lost $10000 in Google Stock, your income now is ($50000-$3000) $47000.

You can also now sell $7000 worth of winning stocks during the year without any additional capital gains.

Chapter Quiz/Summary

1. One way to reduce your tax is to never sell stocks (True/False)
2. One way to reduce your tax is to use a retirement account (True/False)
3. One way to reduce your tax is to not tell the Government (True/False)
4. Is it better to sell stocks within 1 year or after 1 year?
5. One way to reduce tax is to defer your annual bonus to the next year (True/False)
6. What is a good tax advantaged retirement account in the US?

Answers:

1. True
2. True
3. False
4. After 1 year, as there is reduced capital gains tax
5. True
6. Roth IRA / IRA

Conclusion

Dividend investing in times of inflation can be very difficult but it's also a great opportunity. Sometimes all you need to do is to take time to understand the metrics of dividend investing and learn from other investors as well. It has been a great delight putting this piece together because, even for me, it has been a great learning curve. Dividend investing is undoubtedly one of the best forms of investment. Once you have learned all the dynamics, you cannot help but fall in love with it.

We've gone through a lot of different topics in this book. However, there is a lot more to learn in detail about dividend investing and investing in general. Here's a couple of books we've written about inflation investing, that you would find really useful that go into detail on inflation investing.

Inflation Hacking by Kendrick Fernandez

Investing for the Long Run by Kendrick Fernandez

One of our favorite books is written by global macroeconomic strategist, Ray Dalio, who talks about how the changing world is going to affect our world and investments.

The Changing World Order by Ray Dalio

And a couple of other books we loved were:

Bear Market Investing Strategies

Dividend Growth Investing

The end... almost!

Reviews are not easy to come by.

As an independent author with a tiny marketing budget, I rely on readers, like you, to leave a short review on Amazon.

Even if it's just a sentence or two!

So if you enjoyed the book, please head to the product page, and leave a review as shown below.

I am very appreciative for your review as it truly makes a difference.

Thank you from the bottom of my heart for purchasing this book and reading it to the end.

174

Using Options to Hedge Your Portfolio and Get More Passive Income

Think about 'options trading' as just that, an option. It's a complicated for beginner traders, that's why it's an extra in the book.

But if you learn how to use it, it's an additional tool that you can use to generate more passive income and hedge the risk in your portfolio.

In this chapter, we're going to do a brief intro to options and then some strategies you can use to complement your Dividend Investing strategy. If you'd like to learn about Options trading in detail, then we have a book that goes through the entire process from scratch. The book has worksheets and is written with the sole intention of getting you proficient in options trading.

The book is called "The Only Options Trading You'll Ever Need" and you can get it here.

What are Options?

In finance, an option is a contract that allows the holder of the contract the right to buy or sell an asset on or before an agreed future date. The selling/buying price of the stock is determined by the option.

The buyer has to pay a premium on the option to the seller.

A single options contract is for 100 shares of a company. That is the minimum number of shares that can be traded using an options contract.

Options can be very confusing for investors, so this chapter is structured to explain everything that you need to know.

Call Options

This is the most common type of option. This option is ideal for buying, not selling. The buyer of an option hopes that at a future date when they 'call' the option the stock will have risen beyond the strike price. This means that they will pay the earlier agreed-upon price—a price that is lower than the actual value. The investor bets that the stock will increase in value and this is often referred to as 'going long'.

Put Option

The buyer of a put option has the right to sell, not buy, an asset at a given time. This is the counterpart to the call option. The buyer of a put option expects that the price of the asset will have gone down since the contract date. If this happens, the investor sells the asset at a price that is higher than the actual price in the market.

How Are Options Traded?

The Securities Exchange Commission (SEC) regulates the options market in the US. These options are traded on major exchanges. Regulated options are much better to trade in than over-the-counter ones. Over-the-counter (OTC) options are unregulated and are riskier. To trade regulated options, you must engage a brokerage firm which will assist in handling your contracts. There is an options table online that you can then check out to see how well you are doing.

As a new options trader, you must be very careful with your investments. There are a lot of financial risks involved in the options market and regulators prefer that ordinary people do not get in too deep.

The risks involved can be far-reaching, therefore the investor should apply to their brokerage for an options account if they want to enter the market as a retail investor.

Selling Covered Calls

When investors sell covered calls, they have the option to sell their stocks at a given price to the buyer of the option. The buyer pays the seller a premium. So, the seller receives income through call options. Selling covered calls is great for people who own stock that has gone up in value significantly. Instead of selling the stock, they can receive an income for waiting to lock in profits.

Looking at it this way, selling covered calls can be described as a strategy for options trading. This strategy involves selling call options against the shares of your preowned stock. The reason why the strategy is described as 'covered' is that you own the stock and there's no need to buy the stock to exercise the option.

There are plenty of ways to make a lot of money in the stock market, but many investors limit themselves to only a few. Selling covered calls is one of the methods that many investors miss out on. Options do much better than traditional stocks and, to trade covered calls, the starting point is a stock that you already own. When opening the trade, you sell the call option. The buyer of the option is given the right to sell that option at an agreed-upon date. You earn some income when you sell the option. What it means is that the underlying stock is 'out of the money' until the expiration date of the option.

When an option is out of the money it means that its strike price is above the actual market price. If this happens, you get the chance to keep your full income from the trade. However, if the option is 'in the money' and is exercised, you have to sell the option to the holder. Since you already own the stock, you do not need to buy more shares on the open market to have the transaction completed.

Suppose you own 100 shares of a stock that is trading around $60. Let's also assume that you are willing to sell in the event that a 15% increase takes place, to $69 within a space of one month. You then decide to contact your broker so that you can sell at $69, who then enlightens you to the fact that the $69 call option is trading for $1 today. Considering that you own 100 shares, you get a premium of $100 for selling the option, from which you will subtract commissions and other expenses. On top of the $100 that you would have gotten from selling the option, you then agree to sell your shares for $69 each before a specific date within the same month. If your stock is above $69 on the date of expiration, you receive an additional $6900 (100 shares X $69) to the $150 that you got at first. This brings you to a total of $7050. However, if your stock is below $60 on the expiration date, then you get nothing out of the call. This is good because you sold the call to somebody else, and you get to keep the $150 premium. Moreover, your stock remains with you with no further obligation. You can even decide to sell another call option against the same stock in the next month, and you can generate a recurring income stream from the stock this way.

The Advantages and Disadvantages of Selling Covered Calls

Covered calls are a good way to earn income from the options premium and the appreciation of the stock price. This is a good way to accumulate wealth. If you are looking for ways to increase your passive income, this could be one of the good ways to do so. The strategy also helps to reduce downside risks that may affect your finances. The advantage is that you already own the shares under the options contract, as explained earlier. There is no need for you to go out into the market to buy so that the transaction can be completed.

On the other hand, there are some disadvantages associated with the trading of covered calls. One of them is that the selling of covered calls limits the amount of upside potential; when stocks go up above the strike price, you are forced to sell them for a price that is less than the actual worth currently prevailing in the market. In the above example, if the stock goes to $100; you still sell your stock at $69 only. This caps your gains.

One other disadvantage is that if you decide to sell the underlying stock before the expiration date, you might have to buy the options contract back. The transaction costs may increase while, at the same time, limiting your gains and increasing the total losses that you incur.

Selling covered calls is still a great way to earn passive income and to limit the risks that come with holding a stock in your portfolio. This is an ideal trading strategy for the holder of a stock long term. You, therefore, would want to trade in a way that minimizes the risks of losing your money in that stock. Of course, selling covered calls comes with disadvantages, but this should not stop you from trying it out. Honestly, there is no trading strategy that is completely risk-proof. All you must do is to trade carefully and to dedicate yourself to doing what it takes to minimize the risks involved.

Selling Cash-Secured Put Options

This is a great way to earn extra income. A cash-secured put has to do with the selling the option to buy 100 shares of a stock at a lower price. The goal is that the put expires worthless so that the premium is kept, or to be able to acquire a stock at a price that is below the current price.

For example, you want to buy a DBY stock trading at $20, but you think that it is too high at this price. Instead of buying you decide to sell one put at $18 that expires in the next 2 months for the premium of one dollar.

Because this is a cash-secured put, you will have to keep the cash in a money market account. There are two things that could happen:

1. You would receive a premium of $100 for 1 contract ($1 premium X 100 shares). Remember than any options contract has a minimum of 100 shares.

2. DBY can fall below $18 before the expiration date, and you might get assigned DBY shares. So, you would be buying 100 shares of DBX for one contract and spending $1800.

Before starting the trade, your brokerage would check to ensure you have access to $1800.

3. If DBY is above $18, you keep the premium, and cannot buy the stock.

The potential profit of a cash-secured put is limited to the premium received. You achieve maximum profit if the underlying stock trades at above $18 until the expiration date. You then have to subtract the trading fees from the premium received. The potential loss is also limited to the difference between the strike price and the premium plus trading fees.

The selling of cash-secured puts is a bullish way of trading, although it is not as bullish as outright stock ownership. If an investor is bullish in a strong way, they would go for strategies like long calls, bull call spreads, and poor man's covered calls. Investors only sell puts on stocks that they expect to stay flat, or to only rise slightly, and not drop too much as well.

When Should You Sell Cash-Secured Puts?

It is best to sell cash-secured put options when there is either a slightly bullish or neutral outlook on a stock. It is great when you have a stock you really want to buy but the stock is very expensive. For example, if Microsoft is at $300 per share, and you want to buy it at $200 per share; you can sell a put option with a strike price of $200.

There are several things that you must consider when determining the perfect time to sell options.

The Risks Involved

The risk involved in the selling of cash-secured puts is only a little less than that involved in outright stock ownership. You should never fool yourself to think that there is no risk involved. There are people who have sold puts on respectable entities and have come away with staggering losses. In the stock market anything goes—ruling out risks is one thing you should never do. Companies, no matter how big they are, can go bankrupt, so the selling of cash-secured puts can go really well if things are going well. But when things go bad, cash-secured puts can do very bad. The best thing to do is to select companies with a strong technical outlook, competitive advantages, and earnings per share that are rising.

The biggest mistake most investors make is to assume that when a stock has dropped, it can't possibly drop much further. This is a very wrong way of seeing things and you should avoid it. A stock can be oversold today, and it can be oversold even more tomorrow.

If a stock goes to zero, you lose the entire amount of the cash secured put. So, in the above example, you would lose $1800 if the stock goes to zero.

Volatility and Implied Volatility

The volatility of the stock market is a very important concept that investors should understand. It is vital for an investor to know the stocks that have the highest potential for a price movement and take advantage when they can. Stock market volatility, by definition, is the range of movements in prices over time. A trade that is more volatile has the potential for significant gains, as well as significant losses.

There are several measures that are used in ascertaining the volatility. These include the standard deviation and the stock's Beta. You will realize that there is no particular set of stocks that is more volatile than the other. We can talk of stocks that are 'currently' volatile because they may not be volatile in the next review, while another set of stocks is. Stocks may be stable today, but still possess great potential to be volatile.

Implied Volatility

Implied volatility refers to a projection on the market with regard to the direction of movement in the price of a security. Investors use implied volatility to forecast the possible changes in prices. They can even use this metric to determine supply and patterns for specific stocks. The way implied volatility works is much of a muchness to historical volatility. The main difference between implied volatility and historical volatility is that the latter evaluates past changes.

The pricing of options contracts is often made easier through the use of implied volatility. It often results in options that have higher premiums. The forces of supply and demand, as well as the time value, are major factors in the calculation of implied volatility. Implied volatility is higher in bear markets and lowers in bullish markets. It does help in trying to quantify market sentiment and uncertainty but is calculated based only on prices rather than other fundamentals.

How Does It Work?

Investors often use implied volatility as a tool for forecasting changes in stock prices in the future. such predictions are done after considering some important predictive factors. Usually, the implied volatility is presented in the form of percentages and standard deviations over a defined timeframe.

When the market is bearish, the projection by investors is oriented toward the notion that the prices will fall as time progresses. For this reason, the implied volatility is higher. This is contrary to what happens when the market is bullish. In this case, the investors look forward to an increase in prices so the implied volatility is lower. Usually, investors reflect negative feelings toward bearish markets due to the increased amount of risk that they are associated with. Another important point to note is that implied volatility is not a clear indicator of the direction in which prices might move. For instance, high implied volatility may imply that the price could move toward any of the two extremes, either high or low. Another possibility is that the prices may also alternate between the high- and low-end extremes. Low implied volatility might mean relatively constant prices as it is unlikely that there may be broad changes.

For an option contract, the implied volatility is the value of the volatility of the underlying instrument which will return a theoretical value when input into an option pricing model.

To simplify the concept, the implied volatility is just the expected volatility in a stock.

The IV Rank

To make implied volatility work for options, we look at **IV Rank** for the stock. The IV Rank compares looks at the historical volatility of the stock over the last 52 weeks. It compares the historical volatility with the current volatility level.

So, if the Implied volatility is 100%, this means that the implied volatility is at the highest in a year. If the Implied volatility is at

0%, this means that the implied volatility is at the lowest in a year.

The Use of IV Rank With Options

The IV Rank helps an options trader to determine if the option prices are relatively high or low. This is important in devising an options trading strategy. In options trading, the IV Rank is the at-the-money implied volatility in relation to the highest and lowest values over the past year. If the IV rank is at 100%, it means the implied volatility is at its highest over the past year. The ideal options trading strategy in this case would be one that looks to sell options as the price of the options is high; and you receive a higher premium.

If the IV rank is low, it's a good time to buy options as the options premiums are lower.

Glossary

- **Blue-chip stocks:** The stock of a large company with a recognizable brand, whose market cap is over a few billion dollars and is considered by investors to be very safe.

- **Commodity stocks:** The stocks of companies that produce and distribute commodities like agricultural products, precious metals, industrial metals, and energy.

- **Dividends:** A sum of money that is paid by a company to its shareholders on a regular basis, that is quarterly, monthly, or annually. It is paid out of the profits.

- **Dividend yield:** It is the dividend per share, divided by the share price. It could be a company's total dividend divided by its market capitalization, expressed as a percentage.

- **Growth stocks:** These are stocks that offer a higher growth rate as compared to the rate prevailing in the market. These stocks grow at a faster rate than other stocks.

- **Inflation:** It is the general and progressive increase in the prices of goods and services in the economy. The units of that economy's currency will buy less than they would if the prices were stable.

- **Intrinsic value:** The value of a stock calculated based on financial models.

- **Options:** A contract that gives the holder the right to buy or sell an underlying asset at a specified price on a specified date.

- **Spread:** A spread is the difference between two prices or yields. It is also the difference between the bid and the ask prices of a security.

- **Utility stocks:** Utility stocks, as the name suggests, are stocks in utility companies that provide basics like natural gas, electric utilities, and water.

- **Value stocks:** This is a stock that trades at a price that is lower than the intrinsic value, making it more appealing to investors.

References

Alvarez, S. (2022, February 20). *What Is The Intrinsic Value Of A Stock?* Investopedia. https://www.investopedia.com/articles/basics/12/intrinsic-value.asp